Color
Capital
of the World

SERIES ON OHIO HISTORY AND CULTURE

Series on Ohio History and Culture
Kevin Kern, Editor

For a complete listing of titles published in the series, go to www.uakron.edu/uapress.

Color Capital

of the World

Growing Up with the Legacy of a Crayon Company

John W. Kropf

The University of Akron Press
Akron, Ohio

ISBN: 978-1-62922-227-1 (paperback)
ISBN: 978-1-62922-229-5 (ePDF)
ISBN: 978-1-62922-230-1 (ePub)

A catalog record for this title is available from the Library of Congress.

∞The paper used in this publication meets the minimum requirements of ANSI/NISO z39.48–
1992 (Permanence of Paper).

Cover image: Modified scan of items from the author's collection. Overlay of aerial view of
American Crayon Factory used with permission of Sandusky Library. Cover design by Amy
Freels. Crayon illustration for chapter opening pages by Rhye Pirie.

Crayon Capital of the World: Growing Up with the Legacy of a Crayon Company was typeset
in Minion Pro with Helvetica titles and printed on sixty-pound white and bound by Baker &
Taylor Publisher Services of Ashland, Ohio.

All photos, unless otherwise noted, come from the author's collection.

Produced in conjunction with the University
of Akron Affordable Learning Initiative.
More information is available at
www.uakron.edu/affordablelearning/

Contents

Introduction

THIS STORY BRINGS together three innovative families who created a highly successful crayon company to make the city of Sandusky, Ohio into the Color Capital of the World. The first moments of the company began as a hot, swirling mixture of English Dover chalk and Sandusky Bay gypsum cooked on the family stove by William Curtis, a recently discharged soldier from the Union Army. His experiments, done at the urging of his brother-in-law, Marcellus Cowdery, created a modern, usable chalk for schools and businesses. Curtis soon added wax and color pigment and realized the value of his discovery—bringing color into the classroom. The discovery, combined with the financial genius of John Whitworth, led to the creation of the American Crayon Company. Since its inception in 1890, the growth of the company became steady and swift to include Prang brand paints and Kroma Color. The company continued on an innovative color spree by expanding its line of crayons and paints, where they were used by children and art students in every state in the country and around the world. At its peak, it employed about five hundred factory workers, salespeople, and office staff in New York, San Francisco, Dallas, and its Sandusky factory produced more crayons per year than anywhere else in the world. The American Crayon Company dealt with the dreams and visions of youngsters all over the world, acting as an industrial fountain of youth filling our lives with color. I found I was no exception. The company helped create my

1

childhood dreams and visions, but I also continued to hold on to the promise of the factory as the Color Capital of the World.

As an adult, I continued to ponder the idea that the world needed a Color Capital. The need seemed to be as strong as ever. For example, "What's your favorite color?" This may be the most innocuous starter question to open a conversation with a child or ask on a first date.

A survey of ten countries across four continents shows that one color—blue—is the most popular answer, whether it is in Great Britain, China, or Indonesia. The best-selling crayons of all time, Crayola Crayons gives us a choice of sixty-four colors. Cognitive experts have shown that we can see about a hundred levels of red-green and a hundred levels of yellow-blue, with thousands more variations for levels of light and dark. They calculate that the total number of colors the human eye can perceive is as much as ten million.[1]

Color is how we express our moods. "I've got the blues." Shakespeare coined the terms "green-eyed monster" and "green-eyed jealousy." Color is associated with national identity. Dutch Olympic athletes always wear orange. A patriotic American is said to bleed red, white, and blue. Color influences what we eat. Comedian George Carlin once did a comedy routine asking, "Where is the blue food?" We use color for shorthand expressions of political parties: "Is that a red state or blue state?" Or a symbol of the Russian Revolution and the Cold War: "Better Red than dead." And of course, sports teams have their colors—the most popular being red.[2] In some cases, universities like Cornell or Denison are simply known on the athletic field as "Big Red."

Color is introduced to stimulate children's creativity. There are subject matter experts who are called upon to tell a story or set the mood for hotels, public buildings, and our homes. Painters would not exist without color. Even writers and poets could not do their work without color. The counterculture celebrates the intense colors of a psychedelic experience. Television network NBC adopted a peacock fanning its tail as its mascot to market their innovation of "living color." Likewise, motels in the 1960s specially advertised on their signs, "All Rooms with Color TV." Four percent of the population has synesthesia, a cognitive condition where letters and numbers are perceived to have inherent colors.

Color is so embedded in our cognitive process we may even forget when we are using it in our everyday language: green thumb, pink slip, blue collar job, white collar crime, yellow-bellied, golden opportunity, white elephant, red tape, and silver screen.

Color is deeply rooted in daily associations. Americans want their paper money green. School buses and pencils should be yellow. Fire engines must be engines red. The first rule of driving school is that green means go, red means stop. Since the mid-nineteenth century, traditional colors at baby showers have been blue for boys, pink for girls. Orange life vests are universally recognized as a signal for safety and rescue. In western cultures, white symbolizes purity and is the traditional color of a wedding dress, while in many eastern cultures, it is commonly associated with death.

The world of color continues to grow with the help of scientists. A team of chemists at Oregon State University who were experimenting with rare earth elements while developing materials for use in electronics in 2009 accidentally created the pigment YInMn Blue. Named after its components—Yttrium, Indium, and Manganese—it was the first new chemically made pigment in two centuries.[3]

Color is our world. And if we have a color world, it should have a capital. This is Sandusky's story of its claim to be the Color Capital.

Selected Family Members[4]

Whitworth Family

First Generation

Jonathan Whitworth (1829–1899) m. **Nancy Walwork** (1829–1903). Engine builder; Jonathan and Nancy immigrated from England to New Jersey and then to Sandusky, Ohio.

Second Generation

John Whitworth (1852–1907) m. **Caroline "Carrie" Curtis** (1859–1931). Financier, general manager, and treasurer of the American Crayon Company.

Third Generation

John Curtis Whitworth (1894–1958) m. **Dorothy Wood Haynes** (1895–1971). Treasurer of the American Crayon Company.

Fourth Generation

Mary Seaton Whitworth (1932–2016) m. **Walter Bruce Kropf** (1927–2017). Daughter of John and Dorothy.

Fifth Generation

Ann Whitworth Kropf (1959–2015). Author's sister.
John Whitworth Kropf (1961–). Author.

Curtis Family

First Generation

William D. Curtis (1824–1913) m. **Caroline Cowdery** (1829–1910). Experimenter in the family kitchen who conceived of the idea of making crayon for school purposes.

Second Generation

Leverett L. Curtis (1852–1929) m. **Anzonetta Broadbent** (1862–1936). "Water Pumper" for his father's crayon experiments and later president of the American Crayon Company.
Caroline "Carrie" Curtis (1859–1931) (See Whitworth *Second Generation*).

Third Generation
Earl L. Curtis (1889–1971) m. **Vera Zistel** (1890–1979). President of the American Crayon Company.

Cowdery Family

First Generation
Marcellus F. Cowdery (1815–1885). First superintendent of Sandusky schools and brother-in-law of William Curtis; he encouraged William to experiment in finding a usable form of school crayon.
John S. Cowdery (1833–1896). President of Western School Supply, the forerunner of the American Crayon Company.
Caroline E. Cowdery (1829–1910) (See Curtis *First Generation*).

Part I
Building the Color Palette—
Three Families Come Together

Everyone is born creative; everyone is given a box of crayons in kindergarten. Then when you hit puberty they take the crayons away and replace them with dry, uninspiring books on algebra, history, etc. Being suddenly hit years later with the "creative bug" is just a wee voice telling you, "I'd like my crayons back, please."

—Hugh MacLeod

Chapter 1
Pink Piano

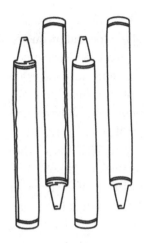

ALMOST EVERYONE IS a snob about something—wine, food, music, or any of the other finer things in life. Me? At the age of five, I was a snob about crayons. I judged the crayons of those few classmates who didn't buy the hometown brand, American Crayons, and thought to myself, "Those Binney and Smith Crayola Crayons aren't any good." American Crayons were the crayons we had at home and at school, and they were the crayons made in the factory down the street—a factory built by my great-grandfather and my great-uncles.

From my earliest memories, crayons were plentiful in our house. My older sister, Ann, and I had the basic eight-pack boxes, plus the wide sixteen packs and the twenty-four packs, both at home and at our desks at school. The largest boxes, with eighty crayons, came with a built-in sharpener and a slanted lid that flipped back to display crayons tightly packed like spectators on ascending rows of bleachers. After a few sessions of coloring, the crayons' neat points were worn down to stubby ends, and some paper wrappers had peeled away, leaving naked, waxy cylinders of color. The well-ordered arrangement became a chaotic, incomplete spectrum.

Ann and I had such an excess of crayons that my father would collect them in plastic buckets and store them in our unfinished basement along with a large spool of blank newsprint hung under the stairs. We would unspool a few feet of newsprint at a time, tear off the sheet in ragged edges, and draw like mad artists on the concrete floor. Ann selected a lot of blue and turquoise, drawing dolphins and flying blue whales and sea creatures with long curlicue whiskers. She used black to outline the hulls and smokestacks of the great ocean liners of the early twentieth century. She added wings to the *Titanic*, the *Olympic*, and the *Normandy* and showed them flying through clouds with the flying whales. For the long, circuitous race car courses I drew, I needed brown and green to fill in trees. When I finished drawing, I would stage races between my steel Matchbox, Dinky, and Corgi cars, with the racetracks running the length of the newsprint. We never cleaned up, leaving loose crayons strewn about and giant wads of crumpled newsprint littering the floor. Sometimes Ann would tape her works to the bare cinder-block walls, recalling the prehistoric murals in the caves of Lascaux, France.

One of my earliest memories was the smell and taste of crayons. After long sessions of coloring, I stuck my face into the bucket of crayons and inhaled the waxy crayon smell to get a crayon high. I drew blue racing stripes on my arms or gashing red wounds on my face. I plunged my hands in the bucket past my wrists and agitated the crayons, pulling up fistfuls and letting them spill through my fingers like a mad miser with gold coins. The flakes wedged under my fingernails and marked my hands and wrists with random colors, making it look like I had some strange skin disease. I unwrapped my favorite colors—blue and green—and bit into each, but they both had the same waxy taste. The crayons in the buckets bore my teeth marks.

One night after dinner, when Ann and I were eight and six, my mother (Mary Whitworth Kropf) said we could draw with our crayons on the dining room walls. The room was large enough to hold a dining room table that seated twelve. I can't remember what I drew, but I know I drew with gusto. Ann drew wild imaginative animals and more ocean liners. My parents joined in recreating familiar doodles from their childhood. Our dining room was illustrated by the entire family, the walls embedded with the American Crayon colors. The next week, the drawings were papered over, forever sealed into the walls of the house.

When Ann and I wore the crayons down to nubs, my mother and grandmother provided more. The supply came from only one manufacturer—the American Crayon Company, made in our hometown of Sandusky, Ohio. My mother's mother, Dorothy Whitworth, known to Ann and me by her grandmother's traditional nickname for grandmothers, "Nonee" (no-nee), had what seemed like an endless supply at her house. Most Sunday nights our family ritual was to drive to my grandmother's white Dutch colonial in central Sandusky where she and her Bedlington terrier, Holly, would be waiting to greet us. My grandmother's full head of white hair almost matched the curly fluff of Holly's coat. Dorothy's correct posture and the white gloves and hats that she wore when she went out impressed upon me that she came from another time. She had graduated from Cincinnati Conservatory of Music in 1919, studying the piano, and during our Sunday visits she would play Debussy's "Clair de Lune" on a pink baby grand piano. She had painted it pink to match the coverings of her sofas in the living room, which hung with portraits of her Quaker great-grandparents.

At Sunday dinners my grandmother would have coloring books waiting with the black-and-red boxes of American Crayons—usually the twenty-four packs. Ann and I would loll about in the back family room, coloring in our books on worn Persian carpets. The tight weave of the wool carpets and their blocks of geometric patterns looked like the grids of a giant city. When I was tired of drawing, I would drive my matchbox cars along the grids of the carpets as if they were grids of a city street.

The early stories that my grandmother told me about the American Crayon Company at her Sunday afternoon dinner table with its white tablecloth and real silverware felt almost like I was receiving a sacrament in church. I was hearing the gospel of the crayon.

■◆■◆■◆■

Three generations before, and a few blocks from my grandmother's house, the Curtis family, a branch of my mother's family, had experimented around the kitchen stove of a small, brick house to work out a formula for a substitute for the brittle chalk that was used in those days to mark on school blackboards. Up until that time, most chalk had been carved out of the cliffs of Dover into blocks used as ballast in sailing ships arriving from England. They were then broken into small chunks and repurposed for school chalk. But it proved brittle and consistently made an unpleasant scratching sound. The Whitworths, another branch of the family, had raised enough money to invest in building a small factory to put the recipe into full production and expanded to develop child-friendly color crayons and drawing supplies for artists. This was the start of the American Crayon Company.[1] The mixture of the two families had been brought together over the mixture of the crayon recipe, and in 1889, a third family was added when my great-grand-mother, Carrie Curtis, married my great-grandfather, John Whitworth.

The American Crayon factory was a brick fortress that sat in the heart of Sandusky, along the Norfolk Southern Railroad line. As a child, I found the complex imposing, with the malevolent tinge of a medieval castle. Yet I was proud that I had some connection to the factory that made crayons. Our elementary school, along with the other schools in the area, would take field trips to the factory to watch the workers boiling wax, adding pigment, and molding and drying the finished cylinders of color.

The black-and-red crayon boxes and steel-cased watercolor sets were something I used in school, and so did my classmates. I took pride in crayons as if I made them myself. Crayons were my birthright. Crayons were in my blood. The blood of family lore matched American Crayon's most powerful primary red crayon in every box.

Crayons sent me down the road to adulthood.

■◆■◆■◆■

Thirty-five years later, I had moved away and raised a family in Arlington, Virginia, a suburb of Washington, DC. Occasionally, I read online stories in *The Sandusky Register*, out of nostalgia and curiosity. Opening up a link one night, I read that the American Crayon factory was scheduled to be demolished. It seemed impossible that the massive brick building, something that had the majesty of the pyramids to me as a child, could be abandoned and demolished. The American Crayon Company had been one of the town's oldest employers since its beginnings at the end of the Civil War. Even the symbol of the American Crayon Company stood for reliability: Old Faithful, the Yellowstone geyser.

In 2001, in a cost-saving move attributed to the effects of the North American Free Trade Agreement (NAFTA), American Crayon's manufacturing equipment was dismantled and moved to Mexico.[2] But before the machinery was removed, the Sandusky factory workers had to train their Mexican replacements on its operation. American Crayon's workers, some of whom had been there thirty or forty years, spent the last days of their careers putting themselves out of a job. After 167 years of manufacturing in Sandusky, the factory shut its doors for the last time in 2002.

The building became more derelict by the year as legal wrangling over who would pay for the factory's demolition pitted developers against one another. Wood floors collapsed, brick walls bowed outward, the mortar crumbled away. "American Crayon Company Sandusky Ohio," painted in white, was still clearly visible from the street. The factory's smokestack remained, an index finger pointing skyward.

One of my artifacts from the factory was a brittle cardboard sign that had been posted on the factory floor, warning in large bold type:

No Authorized Personnel Permitted on the Factory Floor
by Authority of the Company Treasurer, John Whitworth

I also had a few empty boxes from the 1930s and '40s for artists' crayons and a wooden drying rack that had been specially made to cradle children's crayons before they were wrapped and boxed. The wood was an earthy color that carried a faint smell of pigment. I had carted around these artifacts over the decades, but the night I read *The Sandusky Register* story, I realized that out of all my boyhood buckets of American Crayon coloring sticks, I no longer had a single crayon. I went online to eBay and found a couple of listings with pictures. Boxes were now selling to collectors at $18 in *used* condition. I bought five.

When the package arrived a week later, I cut open the heavily padded yellow envelope to see the distinctive black box with white lettering and a red banner with the word Crayonex. These were crayons designed for young school children—fatter in circumference, making them easier for small hands to hold. The boxes proclaimed the brand name Prang with the Old Faithful trademark, Made in the USA, by the American

Crayon Company in Sandusky and New York. Along the side of the boxes, there was a white space for a name. Two of the five had penciled names in block letters, *Kevin B.* and *David Brown.* The boxes were sold with sixteen colors: red, blue, yellow, green, red-violet, yellow-orange, brown, orange, peach, white, turquoise blue, black, violet, magenta, yellow-green, and red-orange. The crayons were more than gently used. The best was a full box of all sixteen with only the wrapper on the brown crayon removed and the tip of the red crayon broken off to a blunt end. Another was in slightly better condition but missing the black crayon. The other two boxes were partial collections of the sixteen colors. The box in the worst condition had no wrappers and maybe only half the crayons. I wondered what drawings Kevin B., David Brown, and his anonymous friends had created for their teachers with their sixteen colors, and how their parents would have treasured those pictures and taped them to the door of the family refrigerator.

The factory also made millions of paint-box watercolors packaged in black, steel snap-tight tins with the red Prang brand on the front and eight ovals of basic colors on the inside: red, orange, yellow, green, blue, purple, brown, and black. The tin lids swung open to create an instant reservoir to add water and dip brushes. Every elementary school student had to buy them every year along with pencils, paste, and a drawstring bag to carry their supplies.

The crayons made in the Sandusky factory were shipped to five-and-dime stores like Woolworth's and to local art supply stores throughout the United States. Kevin's and David's parents and countless other parents bought them to prepare their children for a promising new school year.

The Dixon Ticonderoga parent company slowly moved the American Crayon brand into the background until it was retired for good. It was no longer made in America, and the sad, immediate irony was that the factory in Mexico had transitioned to artists' chalk using the same equipment that had served the factory in Sandusky for decades.

Buying the second-hand crayons was part of a pattern I had of reaching back to connect with the things and places. Artifacts were closely tied to my identity. But as I rolled the different colored crayons in my fingers trying to summon up the old feeling of drawing in the basement, I was reminded there was a spirit of inventiveness combined with business savvy that led to the crayon's success. Why didn't that spirit last longer and the success continue? Why didn't the family that followed have the ability to continue to innovate? What happened to it all?

My mother always talked in glowing terms of her father and "the Whitworths *and* the Curtises." As a child, this created a sense of pride, but as I grew older, I grew tired of the stories. I thought she had an overblown sense of pride and was almost embarrassed. The crayon business was not something she or I had contributed to. They were stories about someone else's achievements. I resented her for dwelling in the past, and I wanted to put distance to that past and distinguish myself based on my own accomplishments.

The older she became, the more she lived in the stories of crayon prosperity. In her early eighties, she became bed-bound, and I relocated her to a nursing home close to my home in Arlington so I could visit her regularly. I would stop to see her on my way home from work and, while she could not remember if she had been served dinner, she could usually recall a story from growing up during her "crayon days" and loop over and over on a certain story.

But ordering the crayons made me want to return to Sandusky to see the old factory before it was gone and maybe sneak into the derelict building and salvage one last artifact, as if I could possess the spirit of the innovation in a physical object. The idea was like an Aladdin's lamp—as if holding onto a brick from the factory and rubbing it could bring back the company and its greatness. If nothing else, a visit to Sandusky might bring me some understanding of my personal mythology of the Color Capital of the World.

■◆■◆■◆■

No one in my family lived in Sandusky anymore. The four of us had moved away one at a time. In 1978, my father was transferred to Birmingham, Alabama, as part of a corporate acquisition. In 1981, my sister Ann married, and she and her husband, a Japanese chef, moved away to Charleston, South Carolina. I kept Sandusky as a home base during college and in 1988 moved to Washington, DC, to work as an attorney at the Department of Justice. My mother was the last to leave in the late 1990s, when she moved to Savannah to live near Ann.

In a strange coincidence, after receiving my eBay order of American Crayons, I returned to Sandusky the next year when my sister died. At a graveside service in Oakland Cemetery, my sister's three adult children—Mary Ann, Olivia, and Daniel—had also heard the stories about the crayons from my sister and my mother. Now they were missing their mother and wanted to see what was left of the factory that was important to Ann.

"Uncle John, we want to see the crayon factory," Olivia said.

"Sure thing," I said. "This town used to be called the Color Capital of the World."

We drove out of the gray cemetery and went in search of what was left.

Chapter 2
Royal Purple

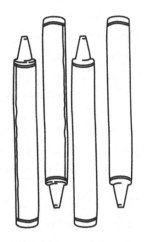

IN SECOND GRADE at Meadowlawn Elementary, our class was scheduled to take a field trip to visit the American Crayon factory. I carried the permission slip home for my parents to sign, thinking I already knew all about crayons. I was going to see my crayon factory and was pleased to think of my classmates enjoying it.

But I was kidding myself. I had never actually seen the inner workings of the American Crayon factory. I had only enjoyed an excess of the factory's crayons and heard the stories from my grandmother.

On the morning of the trip, even before our teachers escorted us off the school bus, a wave of waxy, oil, slightly sweet, and metallic smells floated through the bus—that same smell that I knew from my crayon high from my coloring sessions in the basement. Smell is said to be the most powerful of the senses, triggering the brain's limbic system, which governs emotion and memory. A certain smell can trigger memories in a way no other sense can. The scent of chlorine can remind an adult of a summer afternoon years ago at the pool, a particular scent of perfume might trigger the memory of a grandmother, the smell of fresh cut grass might convey the start of summer. My second-grade brain had anticipated a wash of colors, not the pungency of the crayons. I was not alone. Earl Curtis's granddaughter, who often visited him at the factory after school, said the first thing she remembered was the hot, waxy smell. As an adult,

I heard from family members of former employees like Leah Robinson who fondly recalled the aroma seventy years later, "My Nana worked there in the '50s, she would be 121 if alive. They were allowed to bring the broken crayons home back then, I loved them and their aroma." A Yale University study on scent recognition ranked crayons as one of the top twenty most recognizable scents to American adults.

Inside the brick building, the class passed across wood floors, through heavy doors, and into a large space filled with loud, clacking machines. Much of the manufacturing processes at the factory had not changed for sixty years since the creation of the state-of-the-art factory in 1902. Many of the molds they used still followed the same designs as the originals made at the start of the 1900s by a founding family member, Leverett Curtis.

Massive vats greeted us at the start of the production line like giant kitchen mixers, blending formulas of wax and clay. Separate machines crushed pigments and ground them down into fine power. That day, it was all purple. Powdered pigments were dumped into the doughy mixtures according to the chemical recipe for purple.

The purple dough was then pushed through an extrusion machine into a pressurized mold, emerging like colored pasta or long purple worms. Despite the automation involved, a human touch was still required for critical steps in the processing. Batches of purple wax crayon extrusions had to be transferred by hand from molds to long wooden, grooved boards. (I later found a three-foot length of grooved board among my grandparents' possessions and kept it in my workshop; it was probably over a hundred years old but still smelled of crayon.) Machines then cut the strands into shorter lengths. Some of the extrusions had to be water-cooled so that the wax would solidify quickly. Extrusion machines were limited to one color each week to minimize any corruption of the pigments from other colors. Each machine had to be painstakingly cleaned before it could be used for another color.

Our factory escorts led us along the production line to the packaging process. Women poured uncovered crayons of all colors into a large metal funnel-like machine, feeding them into different channels. The majority of the workers at the factory were women, known to have a more careful touch for delicate, manual tasks. At the bottom of the funnel, the crayons dropped out with wrappers identifying the color.

In separate areas of the factory, we saw the black, metal watercolor tins with the red ball and Prang logo on the front. The cakes of colors for both eight- and sixteen-color sets had to be plucked by hand from boxes of colors and dropped into the templates of the waiting watercolor tins. Each one needed a human eye to select the right color to ensure a complete paint set. Women worked with their eyes and hands every day to complete the watercolor sets used not only by Meadowlawn Elementary School, but also by millions of elementary school children around the country. Molly, one of the women who sorted Crayonex crayons, acknowledged the daily strain but admitted the effort was worth it: "I ask you how many crayons can one person look at in a day? Some days my eyes hurt so bad. I can hardly tell a red Crayonex from an orange Crayonex. Sometimes I ask myself, Molly, is it worth it? Just to make some child happy? But I guess they really need me here at Prang. After all, how would your students feel if a red Crayonex turned out to be orange?"[1]

Our adult guides led us further back in the factory where we saw lots of machines and innumerable conveyor belts. Small, glass jars raced along a production line synchronized with nozzles dipping down and filling them to the brim with brightly colored tempera paint. The speed of the machinery, the way it worked together, was hypnotic, as if it were alive.

We were led away from the assembly line by our guides and into a reception area arrayed with crayons, watercolors, and pastel paints. Everyone on our tour, including our teachers, was given a sixteen-count pack of crayons in the black-and-red Prang-Crayonex box to take home. I wanted to brag to my classmates about my connection to the factory, but the noise and menacing-looking machinery kept me quiet.

The ingredients were now far more exotic than Dover chalk and Sandusky Bay gypsum. The crayons' consistency was a product of wax imported from Africa, India, and South America.

American Crayon's use of color tapped into something much greater—the need for creativity that all of my Meadowlawn classmates expressed. We took our colors for granted as we plucked brown crayons for our horses, and yellow and blue crayons for sun and skies, never realizing that elementary school students before us had not always been so fortunate to create everyday art.

■◆■◆■◆■

Thirty thousand years ago, our ancestors used color in cave paintings of animals in France, Spain, Italy, and North America with only three basic colors—red, black, and yellow.[2] The prehistoric painters found they could mix yellow or red clay or charcoal with water and use the viscous substance to draw their stories on cave walls.

In ancient Rome, a color like the purple we saw being made on our school tour was so precious to produce that it was governed by law. Under sumptuary law, only Emperors could wear purple togas.[3] Later, the color indicated prestige for European and Japanese royalty.

Each color could have its own history book.[4] The number of colors used by artists grew as new sources were discovered in nature. Red came from female cochineal insects or rose madder plants, sepia from the ink sacks of cuttlefish, emerald from unripe thorn berries, and ultramarine blue from crushed lapis lazuli. Color was everywhere, but it was not until the invention of the modern crayon that children and everyday artists had an accessible, easy-to-use medium to create their art.

Like the ingredients of the modern crayon itself, its history is a blend of multiple ingredients combining pigment and wax.[5] The modern crayon was created out of older mediums of chalk and colored pencils. In fact, the etymology of the word crayon is a combination of the French word *craie* (chalk) and the Latin word *creta* (earth).

Among the earliest techniques for combining wax with pigment dates back nearly three thousand years to Egypt and classical Greece, where artisans used a technique called *encaustic* painting, which blended colored pigment with beeswax as a binding element to ensure it would adhere to stone or wood. Artisans used encaustic techniques for everything from decorating warships to illustrations on the walls of their tombs. The Roman Empire also continued this technique, painting marble works of art for funeral portraits, some of which have maintained their color for over two thousand years. However, this was far from everyday, as encaustic painting required highly skilled artisans for work accessible to only the wealthiest aristocrats of Rome. With the fall of Rome, the costly technique was abandoned.

It was not until the eighteenth century that a French archaeologist, Anne-Claude-Philippe, Comte de Caylus, rediscovered the encaustic method through the study of the ancient murals of Pompeii. Caylus's rediscovery allowed him to promote the technique as New Encaustic Art, which initially flourished in Germany and spread to other parts of Europe. While the encaustic method provided the foundation for the waxy part of modern crayon, it was still labor intensive and far from accessible for the everyday artist or as a craft for children.

The other quality of the modern crayon, unlike encaustic paint, is that it is handheld and can be directly applied directly by the artist. Here our crayon history moves forward to look at the development of chalk and pencils.

In the late fifteenth century, Leonardo da Vinci was credited with being the inventor of a colored chalk-like material that today's artists would call pastel, although he admits to adopting it from a French artist, Jean Perréal. Pastels later became more widespread, entering into a manufacturing process in the eighteenth century. Pastel carried forward the binding process by combining pigment crushed into a powder and molding it into square or round sticks, and instead of beeswax introduced a modern chemical called methylcellulose. The resulting pastel allowed artists to blend lines or maintain visible lines and had the advantage of being a portable color medium. Even with the binder, however, the pastel sticks would flake off easily in the artist's hand. It was not until 1795 that French inventor, soldier, and painter, Nicolas-Jacques Conté moved pastels a step closer to the modern wax crayon. In his previous experiments, he had mixed powdered graphite with clay and then formed the mixture into rods to invent the modern pencil. Due to graphite shortages caused by the Napoleonic Wars, Conté set out to design a pastel stick that could be made with a small percentage of graphite, allowing it to be manufactured with ingredients native to France. Conté's mixture introduced clay to the formula and fired it in a kiln to achieve a hard texture, similar to the waxy element of modern crayons. The result became known as Conté Crayons.

It seems unlikely that there is one person who may be credited as the inventor of the modern wax-based crayons. It is more likely that it had multiple parents who worked independently. One is the Frenchman, Joseph Lemercier, who had been described during his life in the 1800s as "the soul of lithography." In 1828, Lemercier started a lithography business in Paris and produced a variety of innovative crayon and color-related products related to his work in lithography.

Soon after Lemercier, Louis Prang, one of the most respected figures in the history of modern crayons, developed his own line of watercolor crayons, which were very similar to the modern wax-based crayon. Born in 1824 in Breslau, Silesia (present-day Poland), Prang emigrated to America in 1850, where he adapted printing and dyeing techniques he had studied to invent a four-color printing process known as *chromolithography*. Prang's system was introduced in the 1860s as the first commercially viable method to reproduce color in print. His passion to use this new technique to make great works of art accessible for students in the classroom led him to form the Prang Educational Company. As part of his business model, he sold several crayon products in the mid-1880s through the early 1900s. He is also known as the "father of the American Christmas Card," using his printing technique to make affordable color Christmas cards.[6] His company would later play a prominent role in the future of the American Crayon Company.

In the United States, an unlikely entrepreneur, Charles Bowley, described as a "jobber-peddler," sold pencils and chalk within a small radius of his home in the Danvers-Haverhill area of Massachusetts, a few miles north of Boston.[7] Like William Curtis, he experimented in his kitchen by refining small clumps of wax and combining them with black, red, or yellow dyes, then pouring the mixture into ice water for fast hardening. Bowley shaped his inventions of colored wax into round and square sticks about five-and-a-half inches long and sold them to local shoemakers and other tradesmen for various manufacturing uses. He also experimented with a toy crayon for children. Bowley developed what he believed to be the first wax crayons in the late 1880s. Both Prang and Bowley would figure prominently in American Crayon's future.

By the end of the nineteenth century in the United States, the first commercial sales of wax crayons coincided with the kindergarten movement, inspired by a group of German immigrants. The movement promoted the idea of developing the whole child, which included creative expression. Numerous companies sought to fill this demand and entered the market, offering various types of wax crayons. Up to this time, chalk, crayon, and colored pencils had not been clearly distinguished, often causing confusion. It was the introduction of a new *ceresin* (a wax derived from a purifying process) that turned the tide to distinguish what we know today as a modern crayon. Eberhard Faber, a pencil manufacturer, advertised crayons in the 1870s and 1880s to American consumers, but most of these were actually what we now call colored pencils. Their version of the *pencil* was essentially a holder for the crayon material for artists to color with. Other pencil companies, Eagle and American Pencil, Franklin Manufacturing, and Joseph Dixon Crucible, created traditional wax crayons as early as the 1880s, as well as the Milton Bradley Company, best known today as the maker of board games. The Standard Crayon Company of Lynn, Massachusetts, also entered the market at about this time and focused principally on wax crayons as its main product.

Chalk was sometimes called "crayon" when manufacturers moved away from the traditional white and added pigment. Chalk was used in various crayon formulations in the 1800s, blurring the line between the two. In the 1800s, artists created "crayon" portraits, since color photographs were not available. The school environment eventually clarified the distinction when, in the early 1900s, paper became readily available to the average student. Wax crayons worked on paper, while colored chalk did not.

Each company sought to create an advantage, jockeying to set standards for crayon configurations and to create distinctive packaging. The earliest packages offered cardboard boxes that had an outer half that lifted off. Companies offered boxes containing twenty-eight different colors and listed the colors on the outside of the box. Smaller boxes of six, seven, eight, ten, and twelve colors were also available with tuck-flap boxes that are still used today. Some early packaging alternatives also included wooden canisters with two pieces of wood that pulled apart in the middle. Over time, the crayon evolved into two sizes: standard size of 3 ⅝ in × ⁵⁄₁₆ and a large size of 4 in × ⁷⁄₁₆.

By 1901, the popularity and demand for Charles A. Bowley's crayons exceeded his ability to keep up with orders. He sought to partner with another company that could handle their ever-increasing production needs. The American Crayon Company had bought out Waltham Crayons (twenty-five miles southeast from Bowley's home in Waltham, Massachusetts). While it is not known who made the first move, American Crayon Company would have been known to Bowley, given its proximity. The two entered into a partnership when American Crayon made him an associate in the company in exchange for acquiring his formula for wax crayons, which increased output and allowed them to debut a catalog of various crayon boxes in 1902.[8] These boxes included The American Crescent Drawing Crayons in seven- and fourteen-color packages; the American Special School and Drawing Crayons in seven and fourteen colors; the American Drawing Crayons in seven and twelve colors; the American Brownie Crayons in seven, twelve, and twenty-eight colors along with a wooden canister containing fourteen colors; the American Perfection Crayons in a wooden canister of seven colors; and the American Banner containing six colors and a pencil sharpener. By the end of that year, American Crayon was selling Bowley's crayons across the country to children and schools.

The following year, a new competitor, Binney & Smith, debuted the Crayola crayon eight-pack in schools. The box of eight colors sold for five cents and was especially made for children.

Like the Cowdery and Curtis experiment, Binney & Smith was another family venture. Edwin and Alice Binney worked with Edwin's cousin, Harold Smith, to create Crayola, and their story was strikingly similar to American Crayon. Edwin was an inventor with an entrepreneurial streak living on the Hudson River in Peekskill, New York, a city nearly the same size as Sandusky. Edwin's wife, Alice, had been a schoolteacher and thought Edwin could use his ingenuity to create something better than what was available for school children to draw with. Edwin experimented on his own and created chalk that was not dusty and did not crumble.[9] The first crayons were black, not used by children or teachers but by carpenters and businesses as an industrial tool for writing on wood and paper packaging.

As a teacher, Alice advocated for children to have color crayons. The color crayons that existed were expensive artists' crayons from Europe, crumbled easily, and some even contained poisonous chemicals. Edwin added his own melted paraffin wax to his mixtures to mitigate these problems.

For colors, Edwin and his team made a list of the basic colors: gray, red, brown, blue, and yellow. He already had black. The team used rocks and minerals to create bright pigments: red iron oxide (hematite) for red, yellow iron oxide (goethite) for yellow, varied shades of red iron oxide for brown, slate for gray, and lapis lazuli for blue. To get the mixtures to blend correctly, the rocks and minerals needed to be ground over and over again to reduce the minerals into fine powders. Some of the minerals did not hold their colors when heated, mixed, and cooled, and Binney had to experiment with hundreds of combinations to find the right results. For orange, green, and purple, he hired chemists to blend various pigments and clays. Binney knew his target audience—children—and from the start looked for nontoxic materials. The team noted the measurements and ingredients of the successful batches to ultimately patent their formula. The mixtures were stirred by hand, poured into crayon-shaped molds designed for children's hands, and then cooled and hardened.

Binney and Smith debuted its first box of eight Crayola crayons in 1903. The crayons sold for five cents in packages of eight colors: black, brown, blue, red, purple, orange, yellow, and green. Alice had the idea to invent a new word for the product—*Crayola*—by combining the French word for chalk, *craie,* with *ola* (from *oleaginous,* or "oily").

Even with the new chemical-based pigments, it was still a challenging process for American Crayon's production team. Tempera paint products included eighteen standard colors in liquid, instant powder, cakes, media mixers, and finger paints. The process of mixing colors for future artists was an art form in itself.[10]

While color paints created challenges for chemists, it activated the most creative instincts in advertisers. To advertise its different color paints, the Fuller Paint Company commissioned an avant-garde series of radio ads that were a combination of short jazz pieces with voice-over artist Ken Nordine. The ads became so popular that the effort evolved into an album of thirty-four tracks, each dedicated to a different hue.[11]

American Crayon even staged a rare national TV commercial showing children dressed up as American Crayons singing, "Whether you're purple like the night or aqua like the sea, yellow like the sun or a bzzz-bzzz bee, you're an American, an American Crayon just like I am—You're an American Crayon just like me, just like we are. We are American Crayons!"[12]

■◆■◆■◆■

Back on our yellow school bus, I examined my black box of Crayonex crayons. In my connoisseur mind, I still thought they had to be better than Crayola. The American Crayon brand maintained a tradition of naming its colors in basic, straightforward names firmly rooted on the spectrum: blue, green, red. Crayola, I thought, tried too hard replacing basic names with elaborate names. I knew what "brown" meant, but "burnt umber"?

The crayon smell was still in the air, but I didn't notice it anymore. Looking back at the factory, I felt like we had learned a secret. Behind the gritty brick exterior, under the monochrome, gray skies of northern Ohio, was an explosion of color. Year in and year out, the factory churned away, creating the tools for child artists to add to the world's palette: red, orange, blue, green, yellow, red, purple, and everything in between.

■◆■◆■◆■

At home, I added my newly acquired crayons to our stash in the basement. Ann seized the opportunity to draw dinosaurs with red and purple color schemes using patterns of diamonds, hearts, clubs, and aces. Many of her other creatures were of her own imagination. She drew a series of standing dog-like animals with long curly whiskers garbed in colorful robes.

I needed a fresh supply to draw pictures of the Apollo rockets, pictures of earth, and space travel. Apollo 8 astronauts gave the world a view of the blue earth surrounded in blackness. Those scenes called for lots of black and blue crayons. Drawing flames coming from the Saturn V engines required yellow, orange, and red. The next year, I probably colored more than I ever did. I needed to draw fellow Ohio native Neil Armstrong setting foot on the moon.

Chapter 3
Gold Coin

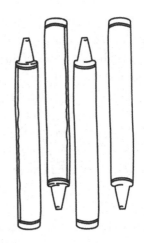

IN THE SUMMER of 1968, I learned a new word: *sesquicentennial.*
Sandusky was celebrating 150 years since its 1818 founding, and that was
the word adults used to mark the anniversary. My six-year-old brain
could recognize the word, but the spelling eluded me. I figured out,
after asking my parents—and with some practice—how to pronounce it.

For the occasion, a special commemorative coin was struck with
an etching of an old side-wheel ship, called *Walk-on-the-Water*, with
smoke streaming from its stack and pennants flying from its masts. The
coin marked the years 1818–1968. My father even purchased a souvenir
Sandusky Area Sesquicentennial stock certificate for me: No. 4081, for
$1, to go with the commemorative coin.

Even if I couldn't spell it, I wanted to know what was so special
about my hometown that people would attach a long word to it. Summer
celebrations were planned, a booklet on Sandusky's history was sold,
and *The Sandusky Register* ran stories on the history of the ship *Walk-
on-the-Water* that brought pioneers to the new settlement. Like most
of my questions about local history, they led to my grandmother. Not
only was she the magical source of unlimited crayons, but I also viewed
her to have a second magical power—like a police detective who had
arranged a wall-sized bulletin board of people and places connected
by threads of relationship, but instead of trying to visualize a complex
gangster organization, her board could be used to trace the interlocking

network of Sandusky's history. An amateur historian who volunteered at the Erie County Historical Society, she handwrote histories of early British blockhouses of the territory in a spiral notebook and did genealogical research.

When I asked her to explain the sesquicentennial, she knew what might appeal to a six-year-old boy—mechanical things like ships, trains, and military heroics. She shared with me that the first settlers came by ship and soon decided to build a railroad leading to the rest of the United States. I was certain there was more, but I only remembered the railroad.

■◆■◆■◆■

On the south shore of Kelly's Island, a limestone rock covered with petroglyphs holds a few clues as to the first humans to enter western Lake Erie.[1] Native American tribes had traveled the freshwater lake, hunting and fishing, and some of their group left their stories on the rock. The land had been kept off-limits by the powerful Iroquois Nation of tribes, who reserved it as a hunting ground. The Iroquois did not keep a permanent presence in the area and over time, bands of the Wyandot tribe slowly moved in to settle along the shores of the natural bay.

French explorers and trappers, including the explorer, René-Robert Cavelier, Sieur de La Salle, acting with permission from the governor of New France, sailed into the Great Lakes with the remote idea they still might find a passage to China. With the arrival of the French explorers and trappers in the late 1600s, the bay's natural attributes made it a popular location as a trapping and trading post. A French map of 1720 shows a body of water called Lac Sandouské (present Sandusky Bay).[2]

With the vast resources of North America, the British soon followed, and Sandusky Bay became a strategic point along the lake. The British built a series of blockhouses and adopted the local Wyandot name for the land as *sandusti*, meaning "land by the cold water." The British named their fortification Fort Sanduski.

The settlement of Sandusky opened up at the end of the Revolutionary War as the first portion of the Northwest Territory, created in 1787 by congressional ordinance. Most remarkable of all was the ordinance did something the US Constitution had not been able to do—explicitly ban slavery throughout the territory.[3]

Ohio had been admitted as a state to the country in 1803 but was still only a handful of small settlements along the Ohio River. Sandusky anchored the westernmost point in what was initially called Connecticut's Western Reserve. Sandusky's section of the Western Reserve was known as "the Firelands" because it was set aside for Connecticut residents whose towns had been burned during the Revolutionary War. The Firelands name stuck and carried on to the present, with schools, hospitals, apartment complexes, and businesses using it in their names. Erie County had the Firelands Medical Center and The Firelands Manor Apartments.

Sandusky and the western islands continued to be a strategic point in the war of 1812. A young American naval officer, Oliver Hazard Perry, built a flotilla of gunboats at Erie, Pennsylvania, and defeated the British near South Bass Island (also known as Put-in-Bay). Perry's famous report of the battle, "We have met the enemy and they are ours!" was his legacy from the Battle of Lake Erie. His victory in 1813 drove the British from the Great Lakes.[4]

With peace on the lake, *Walk-in-the-Water*, the first steamship to bring new settlers to Sandusky, became the symbol for Sandusky's founding, and its image was used on the face of its commemorative coins. The first settlers were New Englanders, a mix of Presbyterians and Congregationalists, who wanted even greater independence from the old settlements and sought a new start. Their religious devotion planted the early seeds of abolition and later formed a critical link on the Underground Railroad to freedom across Lake Erie in Canada.

Hector Kilbourne was Sandusky's Pierre L'Enfant, who surveyed and laid out the street design of Washington, DC. Kilbourne did the same for Sandusky. Kilbourne was also a devout, senior-ranking Mason and formatted the streets to form the compass and square Masonic emblem; Sandusky was the only town in the world to be designed so. Huron and Central Avenue were the arms of the compass, Elm and Poplar Streets the sides of the mason's square. The layout created small, triangular parks. He officially registered the name, Sandusky, with Huron County in 1818, thus marking the city's founding year.[5]

If Sandusky had a George Washington figure, it was Oran Follett, who had been born in the western New York town of Gorham in the Finger Lakes region. Oran's father, Frederick Follett, was a casualty of the Wyoming Valley Massacre of 1778, a combined attack of British and the Seneca tribe on the Pennsylvania settlers. At seventeen, Frederick volunteered to venture outside the settlers' besieged fort to gather food for the families held up inside. He was attacked by the Seneca, scalped, shot, stabbed, and left for dead. Frederick miraculously survived and was nursed back to health by the women of the fort. He carried the scars of his wound and always wore a black skull cap or hat to cover his head. Frederick died when Oran was six years old, and his mother remarried.

At eleven, Follett rebelled against his stepfather and ran away from home working as a printer's apprentice, "a printer's devil" in nearby Canandaigua, NY, and at fourteen, joined the American navy at Lake Ontario working as a "powder monkey"[6] on the sloop *Jones* and fought in the Battle of Lake Erie.[7] Follett reportedly overheard the American Commodore Oliver Hazard Perry remark that Sandusky Bay was the best port on Lake Erie, if not on the entire Great Lakes. The remark must have stayed in the teenage Follett's mind.

After the Battle of Lake Erie, Follett returned to western New York and settled in Rochester, where he began writing editorials for local papers, later starting one of his own in 1819. Four years later, he was elected to the New York State legislature. Oran had a first marriage in 1821 to Nancy Filer, who died, leaving him with a son and three daughters. He married Eliza Gill Ward, and in May 1834 moved west to settle his family in Sandusky. He quickly realized the value of Sandusky's location and chartered Ohio's first railroad: The Mad River and Lake Erie Railroad.

Follett's house was an impressive Greek Revival-style house that he had constructed to be centrally located on one of Sandusky's first streets, Wayne Street.[8] His house was unlike anything the town had seen. Sandusky's early residents would have been impressed with the golden-toned limestone walls and twin curved staircases leading to the front door flanked by Greek-style pillars. American builders had started to use Greek influences in Philadelphia in the 1820s, and Follett brought the style west when he designed his home.

Follett went on to lead Sandusky's growth for the next sixty years as a business, political, and civic leader. He was president of the Sandusky Board of Education, superintendent of the Ohio Board of Public Works, and president of the Sandusky, Dayton, and Cincinnati Railroad. He continued to use his writing skills, serving as editor of the *Ohio State Journal* as a means to fight slavery and build a party of resistance. He would later be instrumental in the development of the early Republican Party and in bringing Abraham Lincoln to national prominence.

Follett was following one of the first pathways west for early Americans looking to leave the settlements of the east. Albany, New York, served as an unofficial hub for Americans moving westward from Vermont, Connecticut, Massachusetts, and Pennsylvania. The Cowdery and Curtis families had followed along with Follett's migration to the new Midwest.

The trail had originally been known as a western fork of the Mohawk Trail that traveled from Fort Schuyler (the area around Utica) through upstate New York to Fort Niagara. At the end of the revolutionary war, the New York State legislature authorized the construction of the Great Genesee Road from Fort Schuyler to Canawaugus, New York, to help settlers reach the western part of the state. Many of them were New York Revolutionary War veterans who were awarded five hundred acres for their service. At the start of the 1800s, thousands of East Coast residents moved west. Histories of the Western Reserve described "Connecticut federalism as the most ironclad variety found anywhere to be found... 'old families' were the pride and the weakness of their respective localities... that the state had shelled over with tradition and family."[9]

By 1808, the road was improved with the longest stretch known as the Seneca Turnpike, 157 miles from Utica to Canandaigua. By 1852, the Seneca Road Company was dissolved, and the company's turnpikes reverted to public roads. Many of the pioneering families like Oran Follett's decided to keep going west. Today's New York State Route 5 follows much of the original trail.

■◆■◆■◆■

From the western end of the Genesee Road, lake boats from Buffalo took more adventurous families further west. Ships started regular schedules arriving in Sandusky, bringing new settlers to the infant port. In 1826, there were 355 arrivals.

Oran Follett wanted to decrease Sandusky's dependency on lake ships as the main connection to the outside world. Nearby Cleveland had access to a newly completed canal, giving it an edge in the early transportation market. Follett decided on an innovative plan using new technology—a railroad.

In 1835, Follett was granted a charter for the Mad River and Lake Erie Railroad after arguing that Sandusky's strategic location could be used to access the rest of Ohio. Sandusky held a ceremony for the groundbreaking of the railroad in the waterfront area now known as Battery Park. The ceremony began with a 21-gun salute followed by a procession of local military groups, railroad president Follett and other officers of the railroad, and chiefs of the Wyandot tribe. General and future President William Harrison served as the guest of honor, turning the first shovel of earth. Harrison remembered the pioneering spirit of the young city and later returned to visit as the Whig Party candidate for president in 1840.

The railroad engaged a Paterson, New Jersey company, Rogers Locomotive, to build two locomotives, the first called the *Sandusky*. Rogers had only built one other engine two years before, with parts of the assembly performed in England and shipped to New Jersey. Rogers had experimented with early locomotives and made several improvements for its *Sandusky* model by balancing the weight among eight wheels and synchronizing them with an external iron rod. This basic design set the standard for locomotives for the next fifty years.

With some small irony, the engine *Sandusky* was transported to Buffalo by way of the Erie Canal and placed aboard a schooner also named *Sandusky*. The engine had been the subject of local interest for weeks, and thousands of curiosity seekers appeared along the route to sneak a peek at this modern technological wonder. When the engine reached Sandusky, it was unloaded at the dock on the foot of Wayne Street and taken by bobsled with a team of oxen to Knight's blacksmith shop at Columbus Avenue and Market Street. After some minor adjustments from the blacksmiths, the *Sandusky* was hauled to the terminus on Water Street and aligned with the gauge of the track. There must have been a moment of relief and exultation when it first fit on the track and the wheels of the engine began to move the new machine. The *Sandusky* was housed in a shed and first put to use in construction of the track, which was completed in 1840.

The *Sandusky* represented a number of innovative firsts. It was the first locomotive constructed entirely in the US (previously, parts had been imported from England), the first locomotive to be delivered west of the Allegheny Mountains, and the first locomotive to operate in Ohio.

The new technology of railways filled an immediate demand. Other Ohio entrepreneurs built their own railroad lines. The Mad River Railroad soon merged into the Sandusky, Dayton, and Cincinnati Railroad. Its railroad lines were considered a rival to nearby Cleveland, which would eventually become a transit point for several national train lines. The Cleveland, Cincinnati, Chicago, and St. Louis Railway, known as the Big Four, formed in 1889 and operated into the first half of the twentieth century.

When Charles Dickens toured America in 1842 giving readings and lectures, he arrived in Sandusky on a Sunday afternoon. He had left Cincinnati several days before and traveled by railroad for the last leg of his trip, which he described as "very slow, its construction being indifferent, and the ground wet and marshy."[10] Dickens ate dinner at the waterfront hotel, called the Steamboat Hotel, to wait for the first ship to take him back east to Cleveland. In his book, *American Notes*, a travelogue of his trip, he offered a grumpy review of his host, annoyed by the man who walked into his room while wearing a hat indoors and by the "funny old lady" who waited on him, ate with him, and then produced a large pin to pick her teeth.[11]

Dickens could not wait to leave. The moment the steamer *Constitution* pulled into the wharf, he hurried on board "with all speed, and soon left Sandusky far behind." As the ship steamed out into Lake Erie, his parting observation about the voyage was that it "conveyed that kind of feeling to me, which I should be likely to experience, I think, if I had lodgings on the first floor of a powder-mill."[12]

■◆■◆■◆■

At about the same time Dickens was complaining about the crude American frontier, his countryman, Jonathan Whitworth, was making his way in the opposite direction, from Lancashire, England. He emigrated as a thirteen-year-old boy without his parents, when he shipped out from the port of Liverpool to Philadelphia, attracted by stories of the new railroads in America, and soon made his way to Passaic County, New Jersey. Jonathan focused early on a trade as a railroad mechanic. In all likelihood, Jonathan probably worked at Rogers Locomotive, since it was the only engine builder in Paterson. Once in Paterson, Jonathan met another English immigrant, Nancy Walwork, and the two were married in 1849 and, in 1852—the same year Harriet Beecher Stowe's *Uncle Tom's Cabin* was published—the couple had a son, John.

Jonathan followed the same path as the *Sandusky* steam engine. The early success of the Mad River Railroad unleashed a huge demand for railroad mechanics in the Midwest states of Ohio, Michigan, Indiana, and territories further west. (This demand might be similar to what we would recognize today as a demand in California's Silicon Valley at the end of the 1990s for software engineers and programmers.) The demand for passengers and freight was growing by the day in the new states. In 1854, Jonathan left New Jersey and moved to Sandusky with his wife and two-year-old son, attracted by opportunities with the new steam engines of the Midwest. At Paterson, he is certain to have heard the legacy of the *Sandusky*. Jonathan soon found a job with a local railroad and would have likely worked at their maintenance shop at the west end of Market Street a few blocks from Sandusky Bay. Nancy gave birth to two more children: Thomas and Millicent.

Jonathan Whitworth brought his mechanical skills to Sandusky and with that, he brought the third and necessary element needed to create the future Color Capital of the World—his two-year-old son John.

■◆■◆■◆■

In 1861, at the outbreak of the Civil War, Sandusky was far from the front lines of the fighting, but Johnson's Island in Sandusky Bay had attracted the attention of the Union Army as a site for a potential POW camp. The island was in the far north, and its natural boundaries limited opportunities for escape. The army leased forty acres on the island to operate as a prisoner of war camp, which was constructed with thirteen two-story barracks and twelve-foot-high stockade walls. In April of that year, the first prisoners were admitted.

The Cowdery, Curtis, and Whitworth men all volunteered. John Cowdery—brother to Marcellus, the school superintendent and future CEO of the Western School Supply—volunteered for the Union Army at the age of thirty-one and served for several months as a private as part of the Hoffman Battalion guarding prisoners on Johnson's Island. He was a third great-uncle, but to a boy interested in history, it meant a real connection to the Civil War.

Cowdery's brother-in-law and future source of American Crayon's intellectual property, William Curtis, enlisted at the age of thirty-six, leaving his wife Caroline to tend to their four children. William served as a sergeant in the 105th Ohio Volunteer Infantry regiment. His unit fought at the Battles of Richmond and Perrysville. A black-and-white portrait-style picture shows a bearded William in uniform sitting stiffly with his sergeant's stripes, rifle with fixed bayonet, and sword. By his stare, it looked as if he had already seen fighting. His gaze fixed the photographer almost as if he were the enemy. William was honorably discharged in 1865 and returned home to his family.

Jonathan Whitworth, my great-great-grandfather, at thirty-six and with three young children, left his job as a mechanic with the Baltimore and Ohio Railroad to serve as a private during the final months of the war. He did not see any fighting.

While the men of the three families volunteered as enlisted soldiers, Jay Cooke left Sandusky to become a financier of the Civil War. Born in Sandusky to the city's first lawyer, Eleutheros Cooke, Jay Cooke went east to Philadelphia for his education. In 1861, Cooke was recognized for his financing skills and was appointed by Salmon Chase, Secretary of the Treasury, as the agent to sell war bonds, raising over $2.5 billion for the Union. Cooke devised selling bonds in smaller denominations to smaller investors, personalizing the appeal that it would pay for soldiers' food and supplies. At the end of the war, General Grant recognized that if it had not been for Cooke's innovative efforts, the North might have lost the war. Cooke later went on to raise money for the Northern Pacific Railroad.

With the war's end, President Lincoln's assassination on April 14, 1865, sent a shock through the country. When news of the president's death reached Sandusky by telegraph, Sandusky Mayor Geiersdorf called for a citizen's meeting at the courthouse at two p.m. as a show of grief. Sandusky's most prominent citizen, Oran Follett, an early Lincoln supporter, drafted a resolution saying that the residents of Erie County met the death of President Lincoln with their fellow citizens of the United States, "with an irreparable loss and demanded Justice upon the heads of the guilty leaders of the present parricidal Rebellion."[13] A large crowd gathered at the courthouse as mourners overflowed the building. The mayor called for businesses to close and churches and other buildings to be draped in black. *The Sandusky Register* reported that almost everyone cried, from old men to small children. Erie County had lost 130 soldiers.

The Lincoln funeral train left Washington, DC, on Friday, April 21. While the train did not travel through Sandusky, a group of the county's residents traveled to Cleveland, where Lincoln's body lay in state at Public Square.

Johnson's Island prison camp was decommissioned, and its fortifications were dismantled in September 1865. The camp left behind a cemetery of more than two hundred confederate officers and men.

In the aftermath of the war, the State of Ohio opened the Soldiers and Sailors Home in 1888 to care for the veterans of the Civil War in Sandusky. The home was laid out as a college campus on one hundred acres including green spaces, a duck pond, library, hospital, substantial limestone administration buildings, and cottages for the veterans. The facility came to serve as a model for other veterans' homes.

■◆■◆■◆■

One other Civil War legacy was to change one of Sandusky's main streets from Sandusky & Columbus Pike to Hayes Avenue. Ohio had produced well-known Union generals Ulysses Grant, Tecumseh Sherman, and Philip Sheridan. Lesser known was a young politician from Delaware, Ohio, Rutherford Hayes, who had joined the Union Army as an officer. He was wounded five times, earned a reputation for bravery in combat, and was promoted to the rank of brevet Major General. After the war, he returned to politics to serve in Congress and was elected governor of Ohio in 1868 and was re-elected to two successive terms. In 1876, he was made president through one of the country's most contentious elections in national history. Hayes lost the popular vote to Democrat Samuel Tilden but won an intensely disputed electoral-college vote after a congressional commission awarded him twenty contested electoral votes. The Democrats agreed in what was called the Compromise of 1877, on the condition that Hayes would withdraw remaining US troops protecting Republican officeholders in the South, and he would not run for re-election.[14] The compromise effectively ended the Reconstruction era, leading to civil rights reversals and the Jim Crow era.

Sandusky honored him by christening a new side-wheel lake steamer the *R. B. Hayes*, which ferried thousands of visitors across the bay to Cedar Point. At the same time that Sandusky & Columbus Avenue was renamed Hayes Avenue, the Curtis and Whitworth families moved in on the street next door to each other. Half a mile down the street was the American Crayon factory.

When President Hayes left office, he retired to his home Spiegel Grove in nearby Fremont in 1881. He would frequently return to Cedar Point and the islands of Lake Erie in the summers. Hayes died at age seventy from complications of a heart attack at his home in 1893. By coincidence, President Hayes had been my sister's favorite President and I found his biography among her books when she died.

Oran Follett, the "powder monkey" from the War of 1812 and leader of Sandusky's early development, died at the age of ninety-six at his home on Wayne Street in 1894. Follett had opened Sandusky's railroad era and had seen the city through the Civil War into the age of innovation. His charter of the Mad River and Lake Erie Railroad set in motion a chain of events that brought Jonathan Whitworth from England to the train builders in New Jersey and later Sandusky. After his sixty years of leadership for Sandusky, Follett was buried at Oakland Cemetery under a modest headstone.

■◆■◆■◆■

Over fifty years later, I still have my sesquicentennial stock certificate and my gold-color commemorative coin. Turning the coin over, it contained the inscription, "Souvenir Commemorative Half Dollar Redeemable at Sesquicentennial Headquarters on or before June 22, 1968." I never tried to redeem the coin and instead added it to my meager, seven-year-old's coin collection. The coin served its purpose—to remind me of ships, trains, and the city where I grew up still intact.

Chapter 4

Dover White

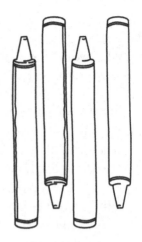

MY MOTHER, MARY, was drawn toward rescuing the hopeless and supporting underdogs. As a child, she wanted to take home broken toys from Woolworth's because no one else would care for them. Watching the movie *Frankenstein*, she felt sorry for the monster as he was chased by the villagers with torches and pitchforks.

As an adult, my mother would take in stray dogs or cats. If she had the means, she would have saved old houses and buildings. Once, after driving by a demolition site in downtown Sandusky and seeing the top of a small church steeple, she pleaded (to no avail) with my father for hours to pay a salvage company to rescue the steeple from the demolition site and haul it to our back yard for display.

Her rescue instinct may explain why she took on a project to save a massive oak partners desk, which had an opening on both sides with the writing areas facing each other. The desk had a long string of crayon lore attached to it. Through my grandmother, she learned about the forsaken desk, located in a downtown office building formerly occupied by a division of American Crayon, the Kroma Company. Kroma was an independent division of American Crayon that provided new coloring products and ideas, mostly targeted at grade-school students. By the 1920s, the Kroma division had outgrown its original site and moved to a sturdy limestone building on Water Street, recently vacated by Hinde and Dauch Paper Company. Kroma's last set of offices downtown left behind office furniture and other unwanted office equipment, including the partners desk covered in a heavy film of dust.

What we did not know was that the desk was a time machine representing one branch of the crayon families that blended together to create the color capital. According to my grandmother, the desk belonged to Oliver Pliny Cowdery, an uncle to Marcellus, the first school superintendent of Sandusky Schools and one-time scribe to the Mormon leader John Smith. Oliver had a complicated history with migration and the Mormons. He was highly literate, and such skills were especially prized in the pioneer areas. Both Oliver and Joseph Smith lived in southwestern Vermont's Rutland County, and Smith had heard of Cowdery's abilities. He persuaded Cowdery to venture west with his small religious group and serve as one of three scribes. The sect transplanted to the Northeast Ohio town of Kirtland. Oliver eventually had a falling out with the Mormons over polygamy and did not follow Smith and his group in their migration west.

Oliver moved further west and used his education to practice law in Tiffin, Ohio, about forty miles southeast of Sandusky, in Seneca County. Connected by the Baltimore & Ohio Railroad, Tiffin was the home of a small crayon factory managed by Oliver's brother, John Cowdery. It was acquired by American Crayon and manufactured up to five thousand boxes of school crayons per day. Oliver soon grew restless, gave up his law practice, and continued moving west to Missouri. Oliver likely donated personal property, such as furniture that was too bulky to move, to his brother John for use in the Tiffin American Crayon factory offices. When the Tiffin factory was later destroyed in a fire, the salvaged furniture and equipment were moved to Sandusky. My grandmother believed, in an elaborate chain of custody, that the furniture was likely used by Marcellus while he was school superintendent or his brother John, who had been the first president of the early crayon company. Marcellus and John would have been my great-great-grand uncles.

My mother paid movers to have the desk hauled out of the second floor of the old limestone office building, which had no elevators, and had the desk fully restored, including replacing the green leather top. She presented it to my father as a Father's Day gift for his den. For years, he would do bills and taxes on it. When I was six and seven, I used to imitate him, pulling out notebooks of graph paper and writing out a sequence of numbers or letters of the alphabet, and after a while I started making up nonsense graphs, plotting nothing at all. I used to climb to the top that was covered in deep green leather matte. The middle section of the partners desk was like a tunnel, perfect for making a fort or hiding. I called the desk doors "secret compartments," useful for storage. To me, the top of the desk seemed as big as the stage of a small theater.

If the lore of the desk was true, it was a symbolic connection to at least two of American Crayon's critical families: Cowdery, who brought innovation to schools, and Curtis, who brought inventive know-how to improving school crayons.

■◆■◆■◆■

As a founding principle of the Northwest Ordinance of 1787, Article 3 declared that "education shall forever be encouraged." The Ordinance set aside a section of each new township's land for the support of public schools. Ohio's Western Reserve, and Sandusky in particular, embraced this principle with enthusiasm and sought to implement the latest in modern education. It was this emphasis that attracted the Cowderys to the area. In the 1840s, the city's leaders saw their future through the creation of a modern school system. Sandusky became one of the first towns in Ohio to create a public high school and wanted to adopt the most modern educational techniques of the day.

In 1845, Marcellus Cowdery had been a lecturer of history and geography at the Western Reserve Teacher's Seminary in Kirtland, Ohio.[1] He had helped organize the groundbreaking school, dividing it into two sections, a Teacher's Seminary and the Institute for Scholars, for those who wished to follow other pursuits. The combined schools were considered a forerunner of laboratory schools for children under age fourteen. Teachers in training were students themselves, learning how to teach younger students. This coed student body trained prospective teachers in a two-year course of study in critical reading, orthography, penmanship, arithmetic, and English grammar. The curriculum included lectures on school management and the latest in teaching methods. The approach was rooted in a groundbreaking philosophy designed to develop both the liberal and technical skills necessary for skilled teachers.

Marcellus captured the attention of Sandusky's leaders when he organized a meeting of the Institute for Scholars in Sandusky. As a result, he was hired as the first superintendent of Sandusky Schools. Marcellus recruited Platt Spencer, a teacher of penmanship who was widely known for the Spencerian Method of Penmanship. The ability to transcribe quickly and accurately was highly prized at the time, and Marcellus launched a magazine of penmanship that was later published in Sandusky High School. The art of penmanship carried forward for over a century. It was not until I was older that I began to appreciate the beauty of my mother's cursive handwriting on simple things like grocery lists and recipes.

In 1856, Marcellus later expanded his influence by publishing *Elementary Moral Lessons, for Schools and Families*, a collection of lessons that could be taught in schools. Typical lessons often had timeless, common-sense overtones: "Live Usefully, Be merciful to Animals, and Do unto Others as you would have others do to you." Each lesson was a short narrative story followed by questions for discussion, illustrations, songs, sayings, and poetry. The book continues to be published today as being culturally important.

Sometime in the 1830s, Cowdery's father, Warren Cowdery, moved his wife and nine children west from Rutland, Vermont, traveling the Great Genesee Road to resettle in a western New York settlement called Cattaraugus. The move was part of one of the first migrations west by thousands of Americans along the same route. The Cowdery family later settled in Kirtland, Ohio. While Marcellus started his professional life as a teacher, his eight younger brothers and sisters received a full education at the institute.

Under Marcellus's leadership, the Sandusky students were assembled, examined, and then assigned one of four grades: primary, secondary, grammar, or high school. The high school curriculum included reading, spelling, writing, arithmetic, grammar, geography, Latin, French, philosophy, chemistry, physiology, algebra, and astronomy. African American students were integrated into the general population of the students—a progressive notion for the time. And because of the great number of German immigrants, some classes were taught in German.

Over the years, Sandusky citizens became ever more devoted to the cause of education and developed a respect and affection for their teachers. Two of the most beloved teachers were sisters Sarah and Eliza Moore, who taught at the high school for over fifty years. When the Moore sisters died, Eliza at sixty-six, and Sarah at sixty-eight, they were laid to rest under a unique double gravestone prominently displayed just inside the gates of Oakland Cemetery—a granite stack of books with one book sitting upright, reaching a total of twenty feet in height. Their former students raised money to buy the marker to honor their memory. The titles on the granite spines and covers listed the sisters' dates of birth and death.[2] It was one of the first things a visitor noticed driving into the cemetery, and my sister Ann, a self-described bookworm, said they were always her favorite of the headstones.

William Curtis's path to Sandusky was similar.[3] He was born in Orleans, New York, a small town not far from where the Cowdery's had settled, and one of the settlements at the western end of the Great Genesee Road near Rochester, New York. Curtis's parents had been born to farming families in Connecticut at the end of the 1700s, and the family kept moving west. William must have felt his parents' urge to keep moving when he left Orleans and settled south of Sandusky. He started a small farm where, according to family lore, he hid runaway slaves on their route to Canada. William Curtis married Marcellus's Cowdery's sister Caroline in 1851, in Sandusky. The pair had five children in twenty years: Leverett, Howard, Caroline, Mary, and Carol. The two families were now connected, bringing together Cowdery's education background and Curtis's hidden talent for innovation. The mixture would not yield results until after the Civil War.

■◆■◆■◆■

With the war behind them, the citizens of Sandusky were united in a renewed focus on education. In 1866, Marcellus campaigned for a levy to build a new, modern high school. The voters approved it, building the school downtown, facing Washington Park. The stately four-story building, constructed with local limestone, was worthy of any eastern university.

Marcellus Cowdery, who continued to lead Sandusky Schools, connected two worlds—education and innovation. He was considered an educational innovator, having learned new modern methods of teaching in Kirtland, and wanted to modernize teaching tools to improve education. He was shocked by the sound made by the gritty chalk used in the Sandusky schools, a carryover from their pioneer days. Teachers and students began each day with the screech of unrefined lumps of chalk scraping across blackboards.

The chalk blocks had been roughly fashioned from Dover Cliff chalk, which was used as ballast in the sailing ships arriving from England in the 1700s and 1800s. The Cowdery and Curtis families who first emigrated from England would have taken passage on the same ships that carried Dover chalk deep in their holds. Even though school blackboards had been around for centuries, the Dover chalk used to mark them contained flint and other gritty material that made writing difficult and damaged the blackboards. There was little refinement from where it was quarried, and the chalk remained largely unchanged from the single-celled algae that formed a sediment on the ocean floor compounded over millions of years.

Marcellus had grown into a commanding figure with an intense stare and a flowing salt-and-pepper beard. When he turned to his brother-in-law, William Curtis, who had recently been discharged from the Union Army, to see what he could do to improve the quality of the crude lumps of raw chalk, William may have found it hard to say no. Marcellus considered William the practical inventive type and thought he could find a solution. Listed in the 1860 Census as a "*Cooper,*" or barrel maker, William most likely knew how to plant crops, irrigate the soil, and fix almost anything mechanical on the Curtis family farm.

William had moved off the farm and into Sandusky. Following the urgings of Marcellus, William began experimenting in the family kitchen in their small brick home on Hayes Avenue. William needed a finer, silt-like ingredient as a counter to the unrefined chalk. Marcellus's brother, John, ran a local outdoor nursery located near an abandoned quarry with a deep pond in it, and they arranged to help William access the quarry as his source of water and gypsum.

William, in one of his many experiments, added the gypsum into a mixture of lump Dover chalk and water. Then, he brought the mixture to a boil, poured it into stick-shaped molds, and dried it in the oven. When he shared the white sticks with Marcellus, the samples immediately proved smoother and quieter than the Dover lumps, and they did not crumble. The result was that he had created a chalk free of gritty impurities with an improved shape that fit easily into the hand. Marcellus had his new tool for modern education. William continued to experiment by adding pigments to the chalk. He soon started peddling the early batches to schools and house-to-house.

Although the company's precise birthday is not known, 1865 is accepted as the year the new chalk was born. Marcellus soon recognized that they needed a business plan and brought in his brother, John Cowdery, whom he considered the business brains of the family. John was skeptical about the risk but believed they could make a go of the new chalk if they diversified their products by adding blackboards, erasers, clocks, and other school-related equipment.

Toward the end of 1869, the first actual factory was launched in John Cowdery's root cellar. William's son, Leverett pumped water for the chalk mix from a nearby quarry pond by hand each morning. Besides pumping water, Leverett also moved racks of newly baked chalk into drying areas of the factory and oversaw the boiling and baking. His duties quickly transitioned into factory manager, in charge of all production. A sharp line of demarcation is said to have developed, with William Curtis running the factory's operations and John Cowdery managing business matters. William continued his experiments, adding color pigments to the chalk. The inspiration of color might have been a desire to express something joyful in reaction to the bleak years he spent during his time in the Civil War.

The Curtis-Cowdery start-up first held itself out as J. S. Cowdery Manufacturer and met with early success marketing to schools in Ohio. John Cowdery, seeing the demand for their product outside the classroom, expanded the product line to include tailor's chalk for marking fabric and carpenter's chalk for marking building materials.

In 1874, John Cowdery used the fledgling company's success to finance the construction of a new factory a few blocks from the family home on Hayes Avenue, and production moved out of the Cowdery root cellar. One of the first new products to come out of the factory was known as 888, or railroad crayons. The black crayons became popular for railroad surveyors to mark critical points on the rails and for freight conductors to mark train cargoes. The 888 crayon was insoluble, whereas ordinary chalk would be washed off by a rainstorm. The company's timing could not have been better. Five years earlier, the golden spike was driven into the ground at Promontory, Utah, completing the first transcontinental railroad by connecting the last open link between Omaha Nebraska and Oakland, California. Railroads were the country's fastest growing industry, and J. S. Cowdery worked around the clock to keep up with orders.

Confident the railroad industry would be a reliable customer, Cowdery turned his attention to what he saw as the company's future— education. Without question, Marcellus's influence played a key role. The company renamed itself Western School Supply (West seemed to be shorthand for the Midwest), highlighting its commitment to begin selling educational products to public schools and universities.

Sales expanded into the schools of the Ohio Valley and beyond. American missionaries carried Western School's chalk to nearly every continent as an effective, portable means of teaching new students. Some years after the first missionary schools were established in Africa, Mr. Kalu Kuloka, one of the students who later became a teacher, traveled to the United States, and paid a visit to the Western School Supply factory. Kuloka wanted to express his gratitude for the improvement the chalk had made for his school, something the younger pupils called "the magic stick."[4]

With the company competing for sales in the Pittsburgh schools, the Cowderys and Curtises ran into a startling discovery. They met competition from the Parmenter Crayon Company of Waltham, Massachusetts. Unknown to Cowdery, Parmenter had started making an improved chalk in 1835. Zenas Parmenter had entered into a business partnership with Dr. Francis Field, a successful dentist living in Waltham, an old Yankee town ten miles northeast of Boston on the Charles River. Parmenter and Field, not Curtis, held bragging rights to the first effective blackboard chalk. Parmenter's beginnings were strikingly similar to Western School Supply's, using raw Dover chalk mixed with other minerals and baked in the family oven. Dr. Field arranged for a local machinist to make wooden molds used to form his chalk. His blackboard crayons were described as grit-free and soon became popular with professors and students at nearby Harvard College.

The parallel experiments, thirty years apart in Massachusetts and Ohio, were unknown to Field and Curtis. Maybe the same inventive spirit of Waltham had carried itself westward like a seedpod blown by the winds to plant itself in the Midwest.

In 1885, Marcellus died at the age of seventy. At the time of his death, the company employed forty employees and had carved out a firm niche selling its innovative product to schools and railroads. One hundred years later, the State of Ohio recognized his groundbreaking achievements through an annual statewide award made in his name— the Marcellus F. Cowdery Educator of the Year Award. The pioneering educator, who had introduced modern teaching methods to schools and sparked his brother-in-law William's inventiveness, was buried in Sandusky's Oakland Cemetery.

■◆■◆■◆■

The Cowdery desk remained the centerpiece of my father's den in our house until we moved away in 1974. My parents later divorced, and the desk stayed with my father through a series of moves. Some fifty years after it had been restored, the desk was passed down to me. I wondered if Marcellus had used it for any of this time writing *Elementary Moral Lessons for Schools and Families.* I invested the money to have it cleaned and waxed and replaced the leather top. When I brought the desk in to be restored, Dave, the owner of the furniture restoration shop, remarked, "This desk looks like it has seen some history."

Chapter 5
Red-Blooded American Stock

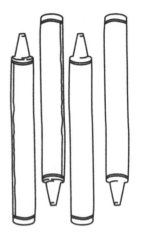

A WEEK AFTER third grade let out for summer vacation, there was a lot of somber activity at our house for what I thought should have been a carefree June afternoon. I watched my parents unload my grandmother's possessions from my father's blue Ford LTD and unpack them in our garage: dark wood furniture, boxes of documents, stock certificates, hundreds of handwritten letters. The stacks increased to the point where my father had to relocate his car from the garage. I was curious about it all but hung back, listening to my parents talk about where they could store everything. While they were occupied with unloading, an accordion file of documents captured my interest, filled with what looked like large sheets of colored paper money with intricate borders of red, blue, green, and gold, and detailed pictures of factories. Each one had a dollar value printed prominently in the corner. I didn't know it at the time, but the majority of them were shares of penny stocks of companies long gone. One sepia-toned certificate, engraved with a stately manor, complete with multiple automobiles, listed the name Pico Park.[1] When I learned that these were stock certificates, representing ownership in different companies, I wanted stock certificates of my own—in the American Crayon Company.

I yearned to be part of the crayon company since those Sunday dinners early in my childhood when my grandmother regaled us with stories about the company. I believed, if my great-grandfather and my grandfather had worked with crayons, it was only natural that I would eventually play a role in the crayon factory's history, too. I turned to my mother; surely it was time for her to start working at American Crayon? I was certain I could work there, too. I asked her how my grandfather had been an owner in the company. It seemed pretty simple to me; all I had to do was get some of the stock certificates in the boxes in the garage.

I pestered my parents for years for shares of American Crayon, the way some of my friends would have hounded their parents for a BB gun or a minibike. My persistence finally paid off, and I eventually received a gift of ten shares of Dixon Crucible stock. The shares had to be processed with the help of an attorney through a special law called the Uniform Gift to Minors Act (UGMA), which held the stocks in my mother's name until I was eighteen years old. (With the amount of effort it took to make the transfer, only later did I understand why my parents were reluctant to go through with the process.) I did not understand the technicalities, but by the time I was twelve years old, I was receiving mail addressed to me by name from the Joseph Dixon Crucible Company regarding my shares of stock. I read about stock and learned that Dixon Crucible was traded on the over-the-counter market and managed my investment by electing to enroll in an automatic dividend reinvestment plan. The pennies of dividends Dixon Crucible stock paid would be reinvested into a fund to buy more.

To me, stock certificates were like family trees, but for companies. A file of certificates was rich with the histories of the company's owners, and detailed when their ownership began. Their personalities, their interests, and their willingness to take risks were all revealed from the certificates. There were certificates of American Crayon, but also many more obscure automobile companies and mining companies. The investments I studied in the file showed the Whitworth family was willing to take risks.

As I learned later, small start-up companies could raise money by making a public offering of stock. My grade-school interest in stocks developed into an answer to the ubiquitous question, "What do you want to do when you grow up?" I went through a period where I answered the question by saying, "I want to be a stockbroker." My great-grandfather, John Whitworth, knew the power of stock offerings and used them to fund the creation of the American Crayon Company. He did this with only a middle school education.

Only a few years older than when I was when I received my first ten Dixon Crucible shares, my great-grandfather, the son of a railroad mechanic for the Baltimore and Ohio Railroad, launched his career. Even though Sandusky was home to a first-rate public high school, it was still common for boys in their mid-teens to abandon their formal education for an apprenticeship, and my great-grandfather was no exception, apprenticing as a grocery-store shopkeeper. The year was 1870, a time when approximately half of the nation's children received no formal education whatsoever.

In the grocery business, my great-grandfather learned purchasing, bookkeeping, and customer service. A quick study, he soon became the co-owner of Whitworth and Free, his grocery store, and later Whitworth & Quinn, located in downtown Sandusky.

He later sold his share in Whitworth & Quinn. Based on his business reputation and strong civic connections, the newly formed Sandusky Citizens Bank hired him as its president where he served for twelve years, later moving on to lead other ventures, including the Sandusky Building & Loan Association and the Sandusky Telephone Company. His years leading the Building & Loan provided him with an ideal vantage point to observe Sandusky's new business start-ups, how loans and investments worked, and how to finance new ventures.

My great-grandfather's official biography in *A Standard History of Erie County, Ohio*[2] described him as having "careful business judgment," although some of his investments may suggest otherwise. I found share certificates of highly speculative ventures, such as the unlikely named Arizona Butte Mining Company of Sandusky.

His formal portrait commissioned by the bank shows my great-grandfather as a compact, sturdy man with a square jaw and a full mustache generously curving across the corners of his mouth. I did not see any resemblance but, according to my mother, I had inherited her father's and grandfather's broad shoulders.

In 1886, thirty-four-year-old John Whitworth, my great-grandfather, met Leverett Curtis, also the same age. The Whitworth, Curtis, and Cowdery families became linked by the marriage of Curtis's brother, Howard, to Whitworth's sister, Millicent. They did not know it then, but the connection was the start of American Crayon, combining investment expertise with crayon know-how. The close bond would follow them through their future business venture, forging a connection between the families that would last generations.

Three years later, John Whitworth married Carrie Curtis, William's daughter. The wedding was held at the family's home and was reported in the society pages of *The Sandusky Register* as "quiet," attended only by immediate relatives. John and Carrie soon had three children in four years: Mary Caroline, Millicent Elizabeth, and John Curtis.[3]

A year after my great-grandparents married, my great-grandfather partnered with the Curtises and Cowderys to launch an ambitious new business plan that carried more than the usual risk. The plan called for the families to invest their money to acquire the Tiffin Crayon Company in neighboring Seneca County and the Parmenter Crayon Company of Waltham, Massachusetts. The venture combined the two companies with Western School Supply and launched as the American Crayon Company with a stock value of $500,000 ($13.5 million in 2020).

The issuance of American Crayon Company stock certificates were the culmination of education, innovation, and business acumen.

The launch of the American Crayon was my great-grandfather's most important start-up. He mixed Dover chalk with Sandusky gypsum to make an effective new chalk and shared duties leading the company with his brother-in-law, Leverett Curtis.

Sandusky was a full participant in the country's industrial innovation, and the family was inspired by what was happening around them. Local entrepreneurs competed with Henry Ford by building automobiles in their garages; Cedar Point Beach became a testing ground for Wright Brothers–era airplanes; the Lake Shore Electric Railway built one of the country's first electric railways along the southern coast of Lake Erie; and Hinde & Dauch Paper Company created lightweight cardboard boxes still used today for efficient shipping. Thomas Edison was born a dozen miles to the south in the village of Milan, and the locals viewed his seemingly endless innovations with pride.

The family used its influx of cash to invest in the region's new technological ventures. John Whitworth bought shares of The Sandusky Automobile Company, The People's Electric Railway, The Sandusky Grille and Manufacturing Company, The Sandusky Chamber of Commerce Company, and The Suneyendeand Club. His wife Carrie purchased $1,000 of stock in The Sandusky Auto Parts and Motor Truck Company. John Whitworth even formed the Whitworth Corporation, which held shares of The Put-in-Bay Improvement Company. John Cowdery's sisters, Martha and Mary, bought shares in The Ohio Phonography Company of Cincinnati, Ohio. Many of the companies failed, and the stock certificates passed down the generations and into the boxes in my parents' garage.

In 1892, John Whitworth expanded into real estate investments, including a four-story office building in the heart of Sandusky's downtown commercial district on Columbus Avenue. The building was leased to a series of local businesses—law offices, real estate brokers, insurance companies, and a cigar manufacturer.

The Curtis-Whitworth families bought homes next door to each other on Hayes Avenue overlooking one of the triangular parks, a by-product of Hector Kilbourne's Masonic city design. The houses were nearly identical two-story clapboards with third-floor attics and sweeping front porches set off with stately wooden columns. The families later connected the houses with a walkway to shield them from the frigid northern Ohio winters. Combined, the two households spanned three generations, with thirteen Curtises and Whitworths, and one Cowdery. Best friends, the cousins played together every day. Earl and his brother Lynn liked to ride with John, my grandfather, up and down Hayes Avenue in a cart pulled by two ponies while the family dog rode along on John's lap.

Hayes Avenue was quickly established as the main work/life artery for the Curtis-Whitworth families in their personal and professional lives. William and Leverett commuted by horse-drawn carriage the half-mile down Hayes Avenue to the crayon factory. Each morning, when the heavy wooden doors of the factory swung open, they were greeted with the hot, pungent aroma of wax as they embarked on their daily experiments with the lavish world of color.

■◆■◆■◆■

The families' success was suddenly tempered by a string of personal and business tragedies—death, fire, and more death. The crayon factory in Tiffin was destroyed by fire. John Cowdery, the original brains of the company and the last of the Cowderys to serve the company, died.

In 1899, Jonathan Whitworth, my great-great-grandfather, the railroad mechanic who had emigrated from England, died at the home of his daughter and son-in-law. His funeral was held at the family home and presided over by an officer from the Grand Army of the Republic who recognized his service in the Union Army. The man who had come from England as a laborer died in the care of his sons, surely proud to know they had achieved some success in the Ohio town where he had moved the family fifty years before. His wife, Nancy, my great-great-grandmother, who had also journeyed from England and then New Jersey, died soon after her husband.

The most serious blow landed on the afternoon of October 4, 1901. A fire was discovered in the factory's dry room on the ground floor near the boiler room. Within minutes, the fire easily spread through the wood structure filled with chemicals and oils. The entire stock of supplies turned the building into a furnace. About fifty women were working in the factory, and all got out safely, most without their coats.

The city's entire fire department of horse-drawn steam engines and pumpers was called out, but the fire had already consumed most of the building. The firemen could do little but protect the surrounding buildings.[4]

My great-grandfather was interviewed by *The Sandusky Register* the night of the fire and showed a quiet optimism, admitting that the loss was a bad one, but assured his customers that they could continue to fill orders with the branch factory in Waltham, Massachusetts. One benefit of the merger years before was that it provided a large stock of inventory in a warehouse in New York City. At an emergency meeting of the

American Crayon's Board of Directors, the Curtis and Whitworth families made the decision to immediately begin rebuilding a new factory.

My grandfather would have been seven years old at the time the fire broke out. He would have been several blocks away, likely playing with his cousins and must have heard the bells of the fire engines. Would he have been excited at the sound or scared?

The destruction of the factory presented an opportunity for American Crayon to modernize, build state-of-the-art processes, and build a safer factory. The new factory was rebuilt so quickly that customers only learned about it much later. The 500,000-square-foot factory was the largest of its kind, equipped with modern machinery and crayon molds designed by Leverett. The building, constructed of brick and fire-retardant materials, covered over five acres, and was located near the old factory site in the 1600 block of Hayes Avenue, several blocks from the house where William Curtis had experimented with his chalk mixture in the family kitchen. An impressive one-hundred-foot smokestack was constructed of sand-colored stone with a vertical brick inlay of the words "AM*CRAYON." Soon after the new factory opened, American Crayon closed the Waltham factory, leaving only a warehouse and showroom at the Massachusetts site.

If my great-grandfather and Leverett were troubled by this string of setbacks, they did not show it. A picture of a Curtis-Cowdery-Whitworth summer picnic in 1902 shows two dozen family members smiling in the sunshine, the women and girls in white linen dresses, some with bonnets and bows, and the men and boys in summer suits with bow ties. My grandfather, his sisters Mary and Millicent, and the Curtis cousins, Earl and Worth, sat cross-legged on the ground and smiled at the camera, looking mildly mischievous, like acolytes of Tom Sawyer. John and Carrie, my great-grandparents, stood in the corner of the back row, smiling in the warmth of the summer gathering. With the last few years of loss, it must have felt like a rare moment to bask in an interlude of joy. At the end of that year, my great-grandfather was named president of the newly formed Commercial National Bank.

Completion of the new factory came at a critical time. The era of modern wax crayons was started by business rival Binney and Smith's

Crayola brand, which had just won a gold medal at the St. Louis World's Fair in the industrial exhibition. The gold medal was proudly displayed on their distinctive orange-and-green themed boxes—a theme used to this day.

American Crayon and competitor Binney and Smith were at the top of what was called "the Big Eight" of crayon companies. The others were Franklin Crayon Company, Joseph Dixon Crucible, Milton Bradley, the Munsell Color Company, the Prang Educational Company, and the Standard Crayon Company. The industry would soon change and consolidate with takeovers, while others would phase out crayons and return to their main products, such as pencils.

■◆■◆■◆■

With a large modern factory underway, my great-grandfather must have taken a moment to think about his place in Sandusky. He had gone from a grocery clerk at age fifteen to a bank president, to American Crayon Company president in thirty years. He looked west to a place that other Midwestern innovators had started to discover. At the turn of the century Pasadena, California had attracted a list of future household names: Chicago map publisher Andrew McNally; David and Mary Gamble, half of the Cincinnati soap-making team, Proctor and Gamble; Chicago chewing gum maker, William Wrigley; Anna Bissel, daughter of the vacuum cleaner maker of Grand Rapids; and Cleveland newspaper leader, William Scripps.[5] Connected to the rest of the country with the railroad, Pasadena offered Midwesterners an escape from harsh winters.

In 1907, my great-grandfather purchased land at the edge of Pasadena, in the shadow of the San Bernardino Mountains, and built an arts and crafts-style winter retreat, next to a grove of orange trees. The close family ties from Sandusky carried over to Pasadena, with John's brother-in-law, Carl Curtis, purchasing a home for his family just down the street. When the house was completed, it was furnished with Craftsman furniture, Chinese vases, and oriental carpets—the same carpets that I drove my matchbox cars over sixty years later in my grandmother's house.

Sadly, my great-grandfather wasn't able to enjoy his new home for long. He died suddenly on September 13, 1907, at age fifty-five, most likely of a heart attack. The Thursday before, he had judged a baby show at the Erie County Fair, where he awarded a prize to every baby saying, "all babies look good to me."[6]

My great-grandfather left behind a wife, two daughters, and a thirteen-year-old son, John—my grandfather. A simple funeral without music was conducted in the Whitworth family home on Hayes Avenue by the local Congregationalist minister. The day of his funeral, the American Crayon factory and Commercial National Bank were closed out of respect. Among the pallbearers was Thomas Sloane, son of Sandusky abolitionist Rush Sloane. My great-grandfather's cousin, Carl Curtis, returned from Pasadena to mourn with the family.

Glowing tributes to my great-grandfather continued for several years following his death:

> John Whitworth. The kind of business success which benefits not only the individual but the entire community was that which was won by the late John Whitworth of Sandusky. He helped to give that city one of its largest industries, one by which the name Sandusky is known all over the country, and throughout his career was a conservative but public spirited citizen, and everything that he touched was the better for his influence.[7]

American Crayon quickly appointed an interim president, Arthur Spore, who left his executive position with the Lake Shore and Michigan Southern Railroad. Shortly thereafter, however, leadership reverted to the family when Leverett Curtis, who had been the water pumper as a boy, took the helm of the company.

■◆■◆■◆■

My grandfather was twelve years old when his father died and too young to be involved in the family business. He was only a couple of years older than I was when I discovered the stock certificates in my parents' garage. My great-grandfather's American Crayon shares passed down to my great-grandmother. Her brother, thirty-five-year-old Carl Curtis, who had already moved from Sandusky to Pasadena, managed her stake in the company for her. My mother's recollection was that Uncle Carl, who took up the hobby of breeding Russian Wolfhounds, had expensive taste. Carl established a bigger-than-life presence for American Crayon, renting offices in downtown Los Angeles filled with Persian carpets and antiques.

At forty-nine, my great-grandmother and her three teenage children moved into the Pasadena house, perhaps hoping the move from Sandusky to the desert air of Southern California might help the family think about a new beginning. My grandfather regularly traveled between Sandusky's cold lake climate and sunny Pasadena's palm trees, graduating in 1915 from Pasadena High School. As a teenager, he embraced the latest innovations in internal combustion engines, much like a high schooler might have tinkered with home computers in the late 1970s. My grandfather enrolled at California Institute of Technology (Caltech). During his freshman year, he bought one of the first production motorcycles and tested its limits by driving through the desert up into the foothills of the San Bernardino Mountains. He outfitted a small workshop in his backyard, complete with a foot-pump lathe where he could make repairs and experiment. I even found his name on a patent for a tire and wheel assembly issued to him while he was still a teenager.

At the company's Sandusky factory, the tragedy of my great-grandfather's early death did not stop the growth he had set in motion. The company's all-in-the-family structure proved remarkably resilient. The year my great-grandfather died, American Crayon actively competed against its rivals with an advertising campaign targeted at educators. The company split its efforts between informational art campaigns in the schools and conventional ads in national publications like *The Saturday Evening Post* that targeted schools and art industries.

One of their signature products, Crayograph, offered durable, pressed, wax-free crayons at ten cents a box. Twice the price of a typical wax crayon, the Crayograph's selling point was that it lasted much longer than a wax crayon and its colors were more vibrant. Crayograph developed a loyal following among art students.

Binney and Smith's Crayola successfully launched its brand through a coloring contest. President Leverett Curtis responded to Crayola's coloring contests by launching an educational department in 1912 that initiated a Crayograph contest across public schools throughout the country.[8] The company enlisted members of the Manual Teachers' Association. Among its employees was Florence Ellis, a former art teacher at the Cleveland Public Schools, who led the education work publishing books and materials for art students.

Another of the Big Eight competitors, The Standard Crayon Company, introduced *penny packages*—compact packages with seven, eight, or nine crayons for young children, which sold for only a penny. The penny packages were an immediate success, heating up competition in the already fiercely competitive school market.[9]

■◆■◆■◆■

Leverett Curtis's most ambitious plan for the company was a partnership with the highly regarded Prang Educational Company, founded by Louis Prang, an American printer and lithographer, who published and innovated with color. Prang invented the Artist's Color Wheel, which is still used by artists today. He had also pioneered developments in color printing, which led to a successful line of commercially printed Christmas cards that earned him the honorary title "the Father of the American Greeting Card."[10]

Today, we take the use of color in media and advertising for granted, but at the beginning of the twentieth century, such use was considered revolutionary. P. T. Barnum, showman, politician, and businessman, saw the value of colorful posters as a way to attract attention to his acts. Audiences craved the excitement of color, and Louis Prang satisfied that demand by delivering graphics products that facilitated quick, cheap production.

Louis Prang was a native of Germany who learned to mix colors for printing during his apprenticeship as an engraver and designer. He became involved in the German revolution and reached America's shores as a political refugee following his escape to Switzerland. Prang and his family settled in the Boston area, where he used his skills as an engraver to build a business in lithographic printing. When Prang was unable to find watercolor paints for his daughter, he reached out to his contacts in Germany to import watercolor sets for sale in American classrooms. His German suppliers provided him with bold cakes of ultramarine blue, carmine red, and mineral yellow.

Prang continued to advocate for art education and created a new education company that marketed art in the classroom and developed a series of art education textbooks. His textbooks brought the power of color to life for teachers and students alike, filled with pictures of famous paintings and landscapes that had only been seen in black and white. Prang's books were distributed worldwide. In 1909, he died at age eighty-five, on his way to the world's fair in Seattle, where the Alaska–Yukon–Pacific Exposition was featuring the company's work.

Four years later, the Prang Company ran into challenges with the impending war in Europe. It relied heavily on imported German materials to manufacture its art products and, as war moved closer and trade restrictions increased, the German suppliers were unable to ship their dyes and other chemicals to Prang. The company approached the American Crayon Company as an alternate supplier since American Crayon had been using similar materials sourced from the United States.

The new venture was organized into an independent watercolor company called Kroma Color Company. Located in downtown Sandusky, Kroma appointed Carey Hord as its first president. The product team introduced coloring book drawings on its penny packages, giving children a complete package that enabled them to color directly on the box. The idea was instantly popular, pushing up demand for Kroma products.

At the start of World War I, American Crayon acquired full ownership of Prang, giving the company rights to the well-known Prang brand name. With the acquisition of Prang, American Crayon inherited a publishing and distribution network that provided well-regarded instructional art books for teachers.

American Crayon had also been looking to nationalize its brand—something Crayola had already done. With the acquisition of Prang, American Crayon replaced its original round American logo with Prang's well-known trademark symbol of Yellowstone National Park's Old Faithful Geyser. The Old Faithful logo was a widely recognized and positive symbol that would give American Crayon the brand recognition they were looking for. At the suggestion of Carey Hord, the Old Faithful logo took center stage for the rest of American Crayon's existence.

Ads and brochures summed up the significance of *Old Faithful* as symbolizing

> the beautiful color, originality, promptness, endurance, and unfaltering fidelity. The American Crayon Company, like "Old Faithful," is always true to its task and is to be depended upon. It manufactures and sells upon honor, delivering quality crayons of real merit. The business was established in 1835 and since that time the company has served its patrons punctually, efficiently, and faithfully. Thus the product has become known as American "Old Faithful Crayons."[11]

During World War I, American Crayon kept its focus on art schools and introduced Pastello, a high-quality brand of pastels especially made for artists. The Pastello brand would see the company through the next fifty years.

In 1916, Republican presidential candidate Charles Evans Hughes held a rally outside the American Crayon factory in his campaign against Woodrow Wilson. Hughes could be seen striking a statesman-like pose on the steps of the factory with Leverett Curtis, his son Earl, and two-year-old granddaughter Miriam next to him, surrounded by other officials with a background of American flags and red, white, and blue bunting draped from the windows. The presidential election was so close that year the final result was not known until California had reported in, giving the electoral vote for Wilson (by only 3,733 votes), with the final electoral vote 277 for Wilson and 254 for Hughes.

With the end of the war in sight, American Crayon established a sales office at 200 Fifth Avenue in Manhattan and a factory and warehouse in Brooklyn, New York. The Manhattan offices gave the company newfound worldwide visibility, and the Brooklyn hub gave it easy access to ship products all over the world.

After World War I, American Crayon continued to market new products, including color chalk, drawing crayons, and a line of Prang brand products. The company had adopted Prang's philosophy of bringing creative tools to children at an early age. One of their most popular products was a kindergarten Color Kit that included a set of crayons, miniature coloring books, and animal stencils. Prang's most famous products were watercolor paints in black, steel, snap-tight cases used in schools around the country, including my elementary school, through the 1970s. The company was sending representatives with a letter of introduction from Ohio Senator and soon-to-be US President Warren Harding to Europe, Asia, South America, and Africa to promote its products. The Sandusky factory now employed over three hundred workers, and its salesmen covered every state in the country.

American Crayon's total value was $4.5 million (about $58 million in 2020). The Sandusky factory produced more crayons than any other factory in the world. American Crayon's marketing minds boasted that they made Sandusky "the Color Capital of the World."

■◆■◆■◆■

In 1920, after his honorable discharge from the army and an adventurous cross-country drive with Earl, my grandfather returned to Sandusky and stepped into the family business at the age of twenty-six. He worked in different departments to eventually serve as American Crayon's secretary-treasurer. As treasurer, his signature appeared on the company's stock certificates. My grandfather continued to indulge his hobby, tinkering with machines and buying the latest tools. He used the company's supply of wood for boxes to build his own toolboxes, shoeshine boxes, bookcases, and small, decorative boxes that he gave away as gifts.

The executive office he walked into every day was a large, starkly decorated open space where the president, vice president, and other officers of the company sat side by side at large wooden desks. My grandfather was part of the second generation of the Whitworth-Curtis family to serve as an officer in the company, along with cousins Earl and Lynn, the sons of Leverett. The three cousins plus a fourth, Worth Curtis, the son of Leverett's brother, Howard, took the company into the 1920s.

In 1925, my grandfather married my grandmother, Dorothy Haynes. Dorothy was the only daughter of five children, and her father, Dr. John Haynes, was the chief surgeon and commandant of the Ohio Soldiers and Sailors Home (later Veterans Home). My grandmother's mother,

Olive Ashton, was from a quiet group of progressive Quakers from central Ohio who sent Olive to college, something unusual for a woman of that time. John and Olive met at Earlham College, a Quaker college in Richmond, Indiana. Dorothy and her five older brothers grew up on the grounds of the Veterans home. My grandmother told me at night she used to wait to hear the clip-clop of the horses from her father's carriage on the bricks outside because she knew that meant he was home.

My grandparents, cousin Earl Curtis, and his wife Vera, traveled together by train from Sandusky to Pasadena to see the California branch of the Whitworth and Curtis families. They toured old mission sites of Southern California usually with John driving, the women in modern twenties dresses and the men in suits and ties.

In 1927, my grandmother gave birth to a girl, but the infant lived only a day. Her brief life was memorialized in a small granite marker at the base of the Whitworth marker in Oakland Cemetery. My grandmother was advised by her doctor that, due to complications from the pregnancy, she and my grandfather should not try to conceive another child.

■◆■◆■◆■

As my grandparents were beginning married life, American Crayon launched an innovative magazine, *Everyday Art*, that contained high-quality color illustrations and articles from teachers and educators on teaching techniques. The company recruited Bonnie Snow to lead the publication. Snow had pioneered the Household Art movement focused on schools and had co-authored a seminal book for artists with Hugo Froehlich, *The Theory and Practice of Color*.[12]

The company saw its future in art education. American Crayon was exhibited at the Panama-Pacific International Exhibition held in San Francisco in 1915. A trade publication, *School Arts*, highlighted American Crayon's showing as "the most surprising, the most extensive, and the most interesting display of crayon work ever brought together." Following up on the company's success at the exhibition, Carey Hord enlisted Cy Knouff, a former schoolteacher and evangelist of the Everyday Art concept. He teamed up with Bonnie in the *Everyday Art* promotion, and together they influenced a revolution in the nation's public school art curriculum and art supply purchases. The publication ran from 1922 until 1972.

Through the 1920s, the company grew its intellectual property, filing eleven patents for new types of wax and pastel color crayons, dustless chalk, watercolor paints, and artist paste. It also continued to market products for industrial use, introducing Polar Bear, a nonfreezing paste, intended for use in extreme outdoor conditions.

The company sought to distinguish itself by the quality of its products. The Prang brand carried the highest standards, with quality control inspectors randomly sampling one out of ten crayons and performing lab tests to validate color and composition. Prang's craftsmanship expanded into the manufacture of high-quality art brushes made of selected hair from very fine to full width using natural wood lacquered handles.

The company made its own packaging, building durable wooden boxes suitable for shipping chalk, crayons, and other art supplies that required well-made packaging for their fragile contents. By 1921, the company made over one million maple boxes a year. The boxes were so sturdy that they came to the attention of the giants of the automobile industry. Henry Ford ordered them by the thousands to hold the electric coils that sat in the engine compartment of the Model Ts rolling off his Detroit assembly lines. Ford did not like outsourcing anything in his supply chain and tried to build the boxes in his own factories, but he could never duplicate the quality. Ford continued to buy boxes until the Model T's design changed, and the boxes became obsolete.

Walter Chrysler, one of Ford's competitors, also sought out American Crayon for its work in color paint. In contrast to Henry Ford, who said that customers could have "any color so long as it was black,"[13] Chrysler believed people were bored with black and saw color as a way for drivers to express themselves. He paid a visit to American Crayon's Sandusky office to learn how the company developed the colors for its paint. Crayon companies had dealt with the same issue in the 1870s. American Crayon and Binney and Smith had made only black crayons because crayons were supposed to be for utilitarian purposes, not for artistic expression. When Chrysler introduced an affordable way for customers to personalize their automobile color, it was an instant sensation, and Chrysler's sales skyrocketed. The color innovation was so popular that Ford had to abandon his utilitarian attitude and rush to catch up.

During the 1920s, the company published *The All-American*, a magazine-style newsletter that typically ran forty pages. Its masthead led with "Published in the Interests of the American Crayon Company and Its Employees," and each issue reported information about managers and employees, new products, and notes from different departments (Crayons, Pencils, Boxes, Shipping), reports from offices in San Francisco, New York, and Dallas, notes from the company's sports leagues, as well as poems, jokes, and baby pictures. Regular news of marriages, births, new cars, and work anniversaries were standard. A 1921 column *Gushes from 'Old Faithful'* featured whimsical stories and corny humor ("The American Crayon Company was founded on 'Curtis-y'"). The May 1927 issue reported the details of the Third Annual Banquet of the American Crayon Bowling League at the Elks Club that included a dinner of roast chicken, butterscotch pie, and coffee. Company president Leverett Curtis was in attendance and expressed his pleasure watching the event.

Only two years later, in September 1929, Leverett died at age seventy-seven. He had continually served the company from start-up to its boom period, a total of fifty-nine years. "I was born with a stick of chalk in my hand, I guess," was the way he often talked about his life.[14] American Crayon was still a family company, and there was no mandatory retirement age at the time.

On October 24, a month after Leverett's death, the country was shocked by Wall Street's Black Monday, the day the stock market crashed.

American Crayon had never known a time without Leverett, and now it had to move on. George Parmenter, Zenas's son, was appointed to step in to lead the company through the dark economic days that were about to roll across the country.

American Crayon stock held its value more than most companies and even thrived during the Depression. My mother said several times that during the Depression, her father and the other officers in the company worked hard to ensure that American Crayon did not lay off a single employee.

Innovation continued, with Earl Curtis filing a patent for a method of packaging that allowed the contents of crayon boxes to be inspected without needing to open the box. This saved time from having to stop, open, and close the boxes.

■◆■◆■◆■

In 1932, two weeks after Franklin Roosevelt was elected to his first term, my grandmother gave birth to my mother, Mary Whitworth. The fact that she was born was perhaps a surprise to the family and provided a much-needed source of joy. The year before, my grandparents had mourned the loss of my great-grandmother, Carrie Curtis-Whitworth, who died at the family home in Pasadena. As "the man of the house," my grandfather had been close to his mother after his father died. There had also been the death of their infant five years earlier, with the doctor's warning my grandmother not to try for another child. Baby Mary was born against the odds. With her own first breath she breathed new life into my grandparents' lives.

When I asked my mother about the factory, she recalled sitting quietly in a big conference room with chalkboards and crayons and coloring paper.

■◆■◆■◆■

In 1935, the American Crayon Company marked its one hundredth anniversary, reaching back to its heritage from the Waltham, Massachusetts, house where the first school chalk was developed. To celebrate, the company issued a special edition of its educational publication, the February–March issue of *Everyday Art,* highlighting its history. It also released a new letterhead that was itself a work of art. Across the top was a gold band with the company name written in an art deco script with the Old Faithful logo in the upper right corner. Bands of orange ran down the vertical edges of the Nantucket water bond paper with the company's vision in the upper right corner, "Makers of 'Old Faithful' Products Publishers of Everyday Art." On the lower left corner, the main offices and factories were listed as Sandusky, Ohio, Fifth Avenue, New York, New Montgomery Street, San Francisco, CA, and the Santa Fe

Building, Dallas, Texas. On the lower right were two gold relief medals, the first showing Old Faithful and the years 1835–1935 and the second depicting a rider on the mythological horse Pegasus carrying a child upward into the light and clouds, meant to inspire children's creativity to soar. This was the middle of the Depression, and the cost must have been extraordinary, but I suppose it is what you would expect from a company claiming to have created the Color Capital of the World. The coast-to-coast offices made me think of the stature of the company at that time—mixing in Sandusky with New York and San Francisco.

For its centennial, American Crayon unveiled a series of new products: an improved Crayonex crayon that could be used on paper, wood, and fabric and a dustless Raygold chalk that provided greater visibility in the classroom—the high-definition version of chalk. The company started a line of linoleum blocks with animal and Christmas themes. The blocks could be used with the company's Tempura paints and printed by school students. Longtime chalk brands of Ambrite, Kroma, Pastello, Excello, Hygieia, and Hyga-Color were offered in fluorescent colors. Two new brands unveiled, Dovercliff (a white chalk and clay combination) and Waltham, hearkened back to the company's earliest origins.

American Crayon distribution was highly efficient and made use of the easy access to the Baltimore and Ohio Railroad next to its Hayes Avenue plant. Products were distributed nationwide and taken to New York City's port facilities for export overseas. Locally, American Crayon even outfitted their Packard delivery trucks with an oversized mockup of a stick of chalk advertising the "World's Oldest and Longest Manufacturer of Crayons."

Everyday Art ended with an optimistic prediction, "We celebrate the advent of our second century of progress, 1935–2035."

■◆■◆■◆■

In March 1940, the movie *Young Tom Edison*, starring Mickey Rooney, played for ten days at Sandusky's Ohio Theatre. Given their innovative backgrounds, it was likely that Earl Curtis and my grandfather were in the audience with other Sanduskians who would have enjoyed a moment of pride in seeing the story of their local innovator's life story.

That November, the month of the 1940 presidential election between Franklin Roosevelt and Wendell Wilke, *Life Magazine* declared Sandusky to be "America's City."[15] It profiled the city's industry and the farmland of surrounding Erie County and noted that no president had ever won an election without winning Erie County. Ohio's second-smallest county was the swing county of the swing state. Since the railroad start-up, the city had nearly quadrupled in size with a population of over 24,000 people.

■◆■◆■◆■

On December 7, 1941, my grandmother marked her forty-sixth birthday at home with my grandfather and mother. The Japanese attack on Pearl Harbor reported on the radio that afternoon must have quieted whatever celebration the family had planned.

American Crayon remained resilient during World War II. The day after Pearl Harbor, my grandfather was back at the office signing new stock certificates bought up by interested investors. Earl Curtis was appointed to lead the company as America entered the war. He made certain the company did its part in war fighting. Pilots needed special wax crayons for use in ready room briefings before their missions, leaving marks that could easily be erased and redrawn for the pilots' next mission. American Crayon provided pilots with the special crayons to map out their missions over Germany and Japanese positions in the Pacific.

US Army standard equipment for their armored units included a carpenter's kit with carpenter's chalk like the type American Crayon had made during peacetime. The US military even created a small unit of active-duty artists who painted and sketched scenes from the battlefield, equipped with color paints and pencils, some of them supplied by American Crayon. Thousands of other soldiers violated regulations by concealing art supplies—sketchbooks, pens, and pencils—and drew what they saw. US Army Private Ugo Giannini, who had illustrated ads before the war, landed at D-Day with a small tablet of paper, pencil, and a tiny tray of dried watercolor tablets. He was able to sketch and paint some of the scenes that day and as he fought his way across Europe.[16]

During the war, American Crayon also modified its packing to show patriotic themes, including a set of Color Brite watercolors issued in 1942, showing smiling children in tin-pot helmets and paper hats driving miniature jeeps and tanks and firing toy guns. Crayonex issued a cover showing a likeness of a B-29 for its box of sixteen assorted colors.

Despite the rations of wartime America, American Crayon briefly expanded its offerings in 1943 with a series of wooden toys under the brand names Educational Playthings and Modern Playway. The toys included a series of sturdy fire trucks, boats, and a set of farm animals. Possibly it was the company's stockpile of wood for its box business and skilled woodworkers that allowed it the opportunity to offer wooden toys. In 1943, the company also distributed a series of Uncle Wiggily stories by Howard R. Garis, made available in inexpensive newsprint to encourage children to color the outlined illustrations.

Despite the war, the company continued to attract highly talented artists such as the Austrian born Emmy Zweybrück-Prochaska. Professor Zweybrück was well known for stencil and textile designs and had been writing and illustrating her modern art techniques for American Crayon in Europe. She immigrated to the United States months before the outbreak of World War II, where she served as the Art Director and editor for *Everyday Art* and later directed artistic workshops in the company's New York and Los Angeles studios until her death in 1956.

■◆■◆■◆■

In Sandusky, my grandfather, who had volunteered for World War I, was now in his mid-forties but still wanted to help. With the ranks of Ohio's Highway Patrol depleted by military service, he volunteered to serve as an auxiliary patrol officer. He completed training and was issued a .32 caliber Smith & Wesson revolver and a gold Highway Patrol Badge.

In 1944, my grandfather moved the family into a bigger house—the historic Moss-Foster house. Its first occupant had published the Lincoln-Douglas debates on Sandusky's tree-lined Wayne Street. The Whitworth household held not only my grandparents and my mother, but also my mother's cousin Robert Ashton, my great-grandmother Olive Haynes, my grandfather's sister Mary, and a maid.

With the family's move into the new house, my mother recalled the young live-in woman, Jocha, who was hired to be their cook and house-keeper. Jocha had come from an affluent family in Holland, but they were forced to flee to America as refugees when the Nazis overran the country. My mother remembers Jocha cried all the time, and my grand-father eventually found her a job at the crayon company.

■◆■◆■◆■

When the war ended, American Crayon continued as before and had now expanded its product line to include over eight hundred items. School supplies, premium artist supplies, and industrial products were sold nationally and exported to nearly every country in the world. They even made specialty crayons for marking red-hot metal called Hotmarx and markers used as a humane alternative to branding cattle called Brandum. The company also continued to expand its print offerings by publishing a series of classic children's stories, such as *Little Lord Fauntleroy,* through its Prang division. The company had also prided itself on keeping its crayons affordable during the war, but after more than twenty years at twenty cents for a box of school drawing crayons, they were finally forced to raise their price due to increased cost of ingredients. The products were awarded medals at industry expositions in the US and Europe. After veterans began returning home, Cy Knouff wrote an editorial in *Everyday Art,* titled *Art and Defense,* suggesting the use of art programs as therapy for rehabilitation for post war stress, what would later be known as Post-Traumatic Stress Disorder (PTSD).

The company had started out with a basic, utilitarian product—white chalk for schoolteachers and black crayons for railroads and carpenters. When the color crayons were introduced, American Crayons found themselves expanding beyond the rugged utility of blackboard chalk and industrial markers. The company would now be appealing to the other side of human activity—pure creativity and imagination of chil-dren and artists. Blackboard chalk delivered information in a simple practical method. Crayons and paint, with their endless array of colors, were messier and opened up a freedom of imagination far beyond the simple markings of white blackboard chalk. American Crayon products were used by both the railroad engineer and the six-year-old budding artist.

"Identification is our business," company president Earl Curtis told the local press in a 1956 interview. "And we like to recall that there is almost no field of human activity in which our products do not play a part."[17]

In the midst of American Crayon's success, competitor Crayola started an effective campaign the next year with in-school workshops to provide instruction to art teachers on how to use Crayola products. Their school approach proved effective and increased their share of crayon sales.

Even as it sold products worldwide, American Crayon kept a solid connection to Sandusky. It had earned a reputation as a family company. Not only were the descendants of the founders officers of the company, but employees were treated like an extended family. Sandusky was still a small enough town where a reputation would quickly make its way through the community. On weekly paydays, my grandfather would go to the teller's window at the company's bank and personally hand each employee their wages in an envelope. Dozens of employees had been employed for over thirty years and some even forty and fifty years. It was not uncommon for three generations to work for the company. Husbands, wives, sons, daughters, aunts, uncles, and cousins would remember their families working together. American Crayon had kept employees during the Depression and through two wars. Erie County resident Kim Clemens Troiker recalled that her grandmother Pearl Liphart worked there. According to Kim, her grandmother "always gave us coloring books and crayons when we stayed at her house. . . . I wrote a poem about how she met my grandfather while working there."

Linda Probst, who grew up on Hayes Avenue near the factory in the 1940s and '50s, remembered making friends with the workers at the loading dock. "The neighborhood kids would make a trip to the loading dock anytime we were low on supplies and Pop Schirg would fix us up! We got crayons and paints, even tempera paint later on." She also remembers log trucks would come in on Thursdays and Fridays and they steamed the bark off the lumber to use the wood for making pencils: "Whew what a smell!"

At Christmas, American Crayon sent employees and retirees gifts of fruit baskets and an assortment of art supplies. Earl's granddaughter, Marty, an extended cousin, remembers her grandfather, who had retired from American Crayon, giving her three different art sets made by Prang: another year a set of crayons and art pencils, and finally a set of paints.

During shift changes, the factory's whistle could be heard throughout the county. The whistle not only signaled a shift change for the workers, but residents could plan their day around its high note. In later years, Sandusky's City Commissioners took steps to preserve the whistle as part of the city's heritage.[18]

Up through the 1970s, students in Erie County schools were fiercely loyal to the company. Sandusky High School students would use only American Crayon crayons and paints for their handcrafted signs made to support the Sandusky Blue Streaks at their football and baseball games.

The Curtis brothers and their cousin John had grown up joking and humoring each other in their hours of play on Hayes Avenue. Later, at the company, they would mix humor with marketing and once announced the manufacture of a mustache drawing kit so young artists could draw beards on pictures of pompous statesmen and fashion models.

If there was a key to their success working together, it seemed that there were never any family feuds. There never seemed to be a sense that any of them were harsh or quick-tempered. My mother also spoke of my grandfather as a quiet man who never raised his voice and did not like an environment at home or at work where people argued. A granddaughter of Earl Curtis said she had never heard him use harsh language. She even remembers how he went out of his way to get the local paper boy to save his money.

■◆■◆■◆■

The acquisitions of Parmenter in 1890 and Prang in 1914 by the Curtis and Whitworth families came to an end in 1957. Now it was American Crayon's turn. The company was acquired by Joseph Dixon Crucible

Company, known the world over as the manufacturer of the No. 2 yellow Ticonderoga pencils. Like Warren Curtis, Joseph Dixon had been the inventor and manufacturer for new, smooth graphite pencils, a revolutionary transition from goose-quill pens. The Jersey City-based Dixon Crucible had a pedigree going all the way back to 1827.

While American Crayon had innovated through the 1930s, it had not updated its original 1902 factory that was still coal powered. The costs to maintain it went up every year, and production made do with old equipment. It seemed the arc of their success lasted only two generations of the Curtis-Cowdery-Whitworth families. American Crayon had only lasted sixty-seven years.

■◆■◆■◆■

The acquisition ushered out brothers Earl and Lynn, the grandsons of the chalk perfecter, William Curtis. My grandfather had already stepped aside due to a series of small, debilitating strokes. As part of the acquisition, American Crayon shares were exchanged for Dixon Crucible shares. Old paper for new paper. This opened up one more branch of the corporate family tree.

Leland Spore, the son of an earlier American Crayon president whose family held a block of shares in the company, was appointed president of the new division, and Dixon Crucible management quietly gave him the job to downsize American Crayon staff. The company had innovated and grown through two world wars and the Depression, and now Leland Spore found himself in the difficult position of laying off friends and longtime colleagues. The job wore him down, and he could not sleep at night. To clear his mind, he would often get up and drive around Sandusky with his wife for an hour or two. Then he could sleep.

The downsizing did not come right away. American Crayon workers continued in their familiar rhythms of the family business, with clerks in the shipping department preparing and sending shipping postcards to customers to give them the estimated shipping dates of their products. The company continued to ship crayons, paints, and chalk while the old wooden floors of the old building grew older, absorbing the aroma of the workday's melting wax.

■◆■◆■◆■

In 1958, eight weeks after my parents were married, my grandfather, John Curtis Whitworth, died from heart failure at the age of sixty-two. When I was touring the crayon factory ten years later, I tried to picture him walking the floors of the factory and remembered the sign that said visitors needed his permission to enter. I wondered if he had a favorite color and if, like me, he enjoyed the smell of the wax crayons.

In his will, the Dixon stock was put into a trust for the benefit of my grandmother. The Whitworth Corporation that had been created by my great-grandfather, with offices in Sandusky and Pasadena, was dissolved, and the last ties to Pasadena were severed.

My grandfather was buried in the Whitworth-Curtis family plot in Oakland Cemetery in Sandusky next to his parents and two sisters, Mary and Millicent, who had died in 1941 and 1946. My mother confided to me later that the Whitworths did not live long lives. At the relatively young age of sixty-two, my grandfather had outlived his father and sisters. It might be symbolic, but my grandfather, who had grown up all his life with the existence of American Crayon down the street and later signed the company's stock certificates as Treasurer, did not live to see life under Dixon Crucible.

That same year, Crayola introduced its box of 64 Brilliant Colors. The product was highly successful with school children wanting more variety, and Binney and Smith took over more of the market.

With the new decade, 1960 marked American Crayon's 125th anniversary. Sandusky recognized the milestone by having its park employees design a garden mound in downtown Washington Park with green shrubs forming the words, "American Crayon Company * 125th Year * Color Capital of the World." Color photograph postcards were sold showing the display.

In the 1960s, the civil rights movement was active in Sandusky, and the American Crayon Company worked with local African American churches to create a more diverse workforce. Mary Rice, a member of Sandusky's Ebenezer Baptist Church, recalls working with Reverend Leon Troy before starting at American Crayon. She remembers assembling the eight-color Prang watercolor paint sets, where the individual color pallets had to be placed in by hand and then boxed and shipped. She said there was a daily quota that everyone had to make and sometimes folks made it and sometimes not. Mary witnessed one of the hazards of the job—the threat of fire. One day the Sandusky Fire Department had to be called to put out a fire in where the pigment powders were stored. "I remember the firemen came through the Tempera Paint Department." The powder and the vats of hot wax created a constant threat of combustion. "I'm so glad I didn't have to work with the powdered paints." The risk of fire was a constant threat working with powdered pigments and hot vats of wax. Whenever neighbors would hear sirens, they would often remark the factory was on fire again.

Mary remembers earning money to go to college and later on seeing the Prang watercolor sets in Woolworth and G. C. Murphy. She wondered if they might have been the very ones she worked on.

In the 1970s, Dixon Crucible quietly pushed the American Crayon brand into the background. In 1972, the Prang brand name was heavily showcased in the latest company catalog, highlighting interviews with Prang employees and the dedication to their products. The American Crayon name appeared in a small font on the last page of the catalog. At the same time Dixon seemed to be missing out. Fluorescent colors, made popular by advertisers and pop artists like Peter Max, had become a hot new trend of the early 1970s. In response, Binney & Smith Crayola brand showed it was tuned into the trend by introducing a special-edition box of eight fluorescent crayons, including ultra-pink and hot magenta, all which glowed under black light.

■◆■◆■◆■

In 1984, Bryn Mawr Corporation, which owned condominiums, commercial property in Florida and New Jersey, a New Jersey bus company, and a Florida restaurant, bought American Crayon's parent company. The new owner recognized that the factory needed significant modernization and encouraged the general manager of American Crayon's Sandusky factory, Joseph Linahan, to discuss building a new factory across the street.

By this time, my parents divorced, and my mother cashed in her inherited stock and spent the money without restraint. Within the few years after the death of my grandmother, she had sold all her shares of Dixon Crucible stock and was on the verge of filing bankruptcy. During my freshman year in college, she asked me to cash in the ten shares of stock I had persisted on receiving a few years before.

The sale produced only a few hundred dollars, but it broke the bond of my connection to the crayons and the crayon corporate family tree. The stock that my great-grandfather had worked so hard to generate for the business was gone. No one in the family was inventing. No one was saving. No one was investing. The discussion of a new factory faded from the local newspaper. I took it personally. All that was left were artifacts and stories.

Marcellus F. Cowdery (1815–1885). First superintendent of Sandusky schools and brother-in-law of William Curtis, who encouraged William to experiment to find a usable form of school crayon

William D. Curtis (1824–1913) m. Caroline Cowdery (1829–1910). Experimenter in the family kitchen who carried out Marcellus Cowdery's idea of crayons for school purposes

John S. Cowdery (1833–1896). President of Western School Supply, the forerunner of the American Crayon Company

John Whitworth (1852–1907) married to Caroline "Carrie" Curtis (1859–1931). Financier, general manager, and treasurer of the American Crayon Company

Map of Sandusky, Ohio, circa 1898. *Courtesy of Library of Congress, Geography and Map Division*

American Crayon Company "Old Faithful" crayons, Red No. 212, 1910s

Charles Evans Hughes during the 1916 presidential campaign—exterior of American Crayon factory

Charles Evans Hughes during the 1916 presidential campaign—interior of American Crayon factory

American Crayon kindergarten coloring kit, 1918

American Crayon coloring book page, 1918 (*above and below*)

American Crayon coloring book page, 1918

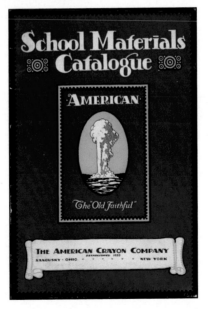

American Crayon Company school materials Catalog, 1920s

Everyday Art, the American Crayon Company's magazine published from the 1920s until the 1970s

Blendwell wax crayons, 1930s

American Crayon truck, 1930s. *Courtesy of the Sandusky Library Historical Collection*

Dovercliff dustless chalk, one gross, tin, 1930s

American Crayon Company factory drawing, 1947, Sandusky, Ohio

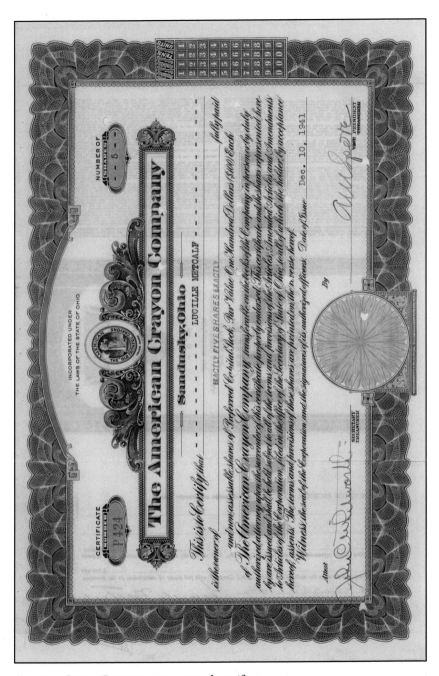

American Crayon Company common stock certificate, 1941

Blendwell crayon tin, sixteen hexagon crayons, 1950s

American Crayons, 64 Pack, 1970s

Aerial view of the American Crayon Company, Sandusky, Ohio, 1956. *Courtesy of the Sandusky Library Historical Collection*

American Crayon Company Factory shortly before demolition, 2016. *Photograph courtesy of Tim Fleck*

Part II
Faded Colors: Bust and Transformation

A box of new crayons! Now they're all pointy, lined up in order, bright and perfect. Soon they'll be a bunch of ground down, rounded, indistinguishable stumps, missing their wrappers and smudged with other colors. Sometimes life seems unbearably tragic.

—Bill Watterson

Chapter 6
Gray Granite Headstones

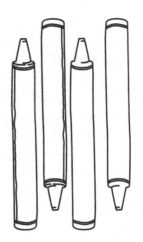

EARL CURTIS, MY great-uncle, died on January 7, 1971, during a severe cold snap in Sandusky, thirteen years and a day after my grandfather died. Earl was the last president of American Crayon before it was acquired by Dixon Crucible. Like John, they both left daughters as only children, the single member of their family to have children.

In June of that year, my grandmother, Dorothy Whitworth, died at the age of seventy-five. She had a general complaint of not feeling well and had checked into Sandusky's Good Samaritan Hospital. Her roommate reported that the next morning she was sitting up waiting for breakfast, let out a big sigh, and closed her eyes as if she had fallen asleep. She had always been in strong health, and I never learned the exact cause of her death. My grandmother's funeral service was held at the Presbyterian Church downtown at the end of Washington Park. It was the largest gathering of people I had ever been a part of. She was buried in Oakland Cemetery next to my grandfather.

Both were buried at the Whitworth-Curtis shared family plot with a headstone the size of a station wagon tailgate: the raised letters of "Whitworth" on one side and "Curtis" on the opposite side. The two families had connected their houses together in life and took the same approach to the afterlife. Individual headstones were rectangular markers the size of a toolbox with inscriptions facing skyward. There were also the markers for John and Carrie Whitworth, my great-grandparents. My grandparents' nameless infant girl who lived for one day, who would have been my mother's older sister, was buried closest to the family headstone. As a child, I thought they should have something colorful to represent the family, like sculptures of crayons in different colors.

After my grandmother died, my mother would visit Oakland Cemetery almost monthly and would take Ann and me with her on her visits along with the family dog, Tasha, our Labrador-Norwegian Elkhound mix. Walking among the markers for her parents and other extended family gave her some form of comfort and a way to travel back in time.

Oakland Cemetery seemed like an outwardly beautiful park turned into a history book. Every family plot contained dates of birth and death all displayed in stone. The information would all be stored here in squared-off plots with granite headstones. When I was a child, I thought that somehow everyone buried had their own network of communication. Later in my adult life, whenever we visited the cemetery, I thought of Thornton Wilder's play *Our Town,* where the deceased residents of Grover's Corners all talked to each other.

In the late 1840s, Sandusky was struck with an outbreak of cholera attributed to contaminated water trapped close to the soil's surface. Hundreds of residents died, and others fled the town. A mass graveyard was created on the west side of town to handle the deaths. Oran and Ezra Follett raised money to treat the victims of the epidemic.

Following the tragedy, Sandusky also set aside land to create Oakland Cemetery located south of town. When it was first opened in 1850, *The Sandusky Clarion* reported on the event as though it were part of a travel feature:

> Those of our citizens who have not taken a trip to the new cemetery ground on Pipe Creek, will regret when once there, that they have so long remained ignorant of so lovely a place. It is the remark of everyone that he is surprised to find so charming a situation for that purpose so near our town.[1]

■◆■◆■◆■

Oakland Cemetery was an alternative world of play and imagination for Ann and me. Most of my school friends and adults saw cemeteries as sad places to be visited only when necessary, but we believed them to be parks filled with stories. We wandered through every section and gave names to graves and markers. We explored different sets of families with their unique headstones, obelisks, and crypts, and gradually felt like we knew the families. There was one family plot Ann used to call the bowling ball family. The central family marker was what looked like a large bowling ball on a pedestal with the word "Father" on it. Around "Father" were smaller bowling balls on pedestals with "Mother" and the names of the children.

The lot across from the Whitworth-Curtis shared plot had family names that became familiar: Beecher, Sloane, and Root—the leading abolitionists of Ohio. Sandusky had been considered a center of abolitionism and the Underground Railroad. *The Sandusky Register* reflected those views in its editorial pages and claimed to be the first newspaper in the country to endorse Abraham Lincoln for president in the 1860 presidential election.

Towering over the abolitionist markers was my favorite marker—the Keubeler family obelisk, the tallest monument in the cemetery. I used to stand at its base and announce to Ann and my mother, "When I die, I'm going to have a monument bigger than this!" Ann seemed to take amusement in this. The Keubelers had once been one of the wealthiest families in Sandusky through their brewery business. If the Curtis-Whitworth headstone was paid for with crayons, the Keubeler obelisk was paid for with beer.

Ann and I would separately visit Oakland Cemetery with my father, but the visits were more solemn. On Memorial Day, my father would take us to Erie County's Memorial Day Parade that started with local marching bands, Boy Scout and Girl Scout troops, fire trucks, and the last rank of the parade—generations of soldiers paraded past from the most recent to the oldest: the Korean War, World War II, World War I, and the Spanish-American War.

When I watched the soldiers march, most were older than my father. I always held my breath for the last rank—a handful of veterans from the Spanish-American War. I knew they were the oldest soldiers and wondered how many would appear—usually it was three or four, some being pushed in wheelchairs. Veterans of Vietnam appeared the final year we attended the parade and were still a new and uncertain part of this line. The parade ended at Oakland's Veterans' Stand, constructed in 1923, in the heart of the old section of the cemetery, where a local dignitary read Lincoln's Gettysburg Address. At the end of the reading, everyone dispersed to lay flowers on the graves of their families.

The parade of veterans made me think of my own family's generations of veterans who had served in the Civil War and enlisted in World War I. I imagined a long parade assembled of Whitworth, Cowdery, and Curtis families marching down the street and assembling at the Veteran's stand. They could start with the oldest, Marcellus Cowdery, by telling stories of their place in time, what Sandusky was like when they arrived, who had the idea for the crayons, and how William Curtis thought to experiment with chalk in the family kitchen. Would they talk about the fire that destroyed the first factory and how they decided to rebuild? Then there was the move to expand the business staking out a presence in California and the move part-time from Sandusky to Pasadena. What inspired that? I imagined a picnic afterwards on the grounds of the cemetery—the older generations interspersed among the younger ones. Two or three consecutive generations could talk to each other, but beyond that they would need introductions to talk to grandchildren, great-grandchildren, and so on down the generations. It would be up to those in the middle generations to pull the family together by reaching in both directions. At such a cemetery picnic, I would have a lot of questions about crayons.

Chapter 7
Lime Green Dodge Dart

WHILE THE FOUNDERS of American Crayon were buried at Oakland Cemetery, the crayon mythology continued to animate my life with the stories Ann and I told ourselves.

Sandusky's location on the Great Lakes provided access to the water and the gypsum mixture that provided the magic ingredient to William Curtis's kitchen experiments. When my mother would take Ann and me to Cedar Point Beach to picnic and swim, we would find Lake Erie as a way to connect with the past. Ann liked to imagine dolphins offshore. She also used the beach to write creative messages to put in bottles and throw them into the lake. During the country's bicentennial Fourth of July, we spent the day at Cedar Point Beach, and she decided to write her own version of a will for the eccentric billionaire and aviation pioneer Howard Hughes who had died recently. She dated the note February 3, 1976, making the following bequests: $500 million each to a daughter and a son he purportedly fathered overseas; $200 million to salvage two ships; $50 million to our grandfather, John C. Whitworth; $10 million each for a Russian violinist, the Academy of the Performing Arts, the Smithsonian Institution, and the person who found the bottle. For reasons known only to Ann, she said the note was written in Quebec, Canada. Ann sealed it, and she let me throw the bottle into Lake Erie. I held it by the neck and heaved it overhand like a World War II German army potato masher hand grenade.

Within a day, the bottle washed up and was found by a nearby resident of Cedar Point who took the note's authenticity seriously enough to enter it into Erie County Probate Court. The will later became the subject of a story reported in *The Toledo Blade* and the *Columbus Dispatch*.[1] The reporter interviewed Howard Hughes's biographer, who doubted the will's authenticity. The finder of the note was quoted as believing it was authentic. John Whitworth lived on through Ann's creativity.

■◆■◆■◆■

I even carried the crayon mythology with me into college. As long as the factory on Hayes Avenue still stood, decrepit though it was, I nursed some kind of hope I might still be part of it.

The summer after my freshman year at college, my father offered to help me find a summer job as a maintenance worker at Sandusky's Vulcan Materials foundry. I was not thrilled with the idea. My head was filled with all the stimuli of my first year of college, and I was restless and depressed after I learned that the girl I had a crush on in the final weeks of the spring semester would not be returning the next year. Taking the job at the foundry felt like I was joining the French foreign legion—it was the appropriate level of misery. In my nineteen-year-old mind, this was what men do in a struggle to forget a woman. I intentionally increased my misery by tapping into a rut of immaturity and drawing on the childish crayon snob kid from fifteen years ago, thinking to myself, "Why couldn't the crayon company still be in the family...why couldn't I get a job working there bossing people around?"

Before starting my summer job, my father gave me a tour of the plant. He wore a hard hat and safety goggles. He suddenly looked more serious as he talked about the temperatures of the metals and the furnace and the equipment that was needed to protect the men working in such hazardous conditions. I had to be outfitted with the same gear. He raised his voice to a dull yell to be heard over the din of the furnaces that smelted aluminum to over 1,300 degrees and explained the inner workings of the plant. He could identify other metals by look and feel—brass, nickel, magnesium, stainless steel, and he knew the temperatures at which each metal liquefied.

In the 1950s, my father, Walter Kropf, fresh out of Detroit's Wayne State University on the GI Bill, was drawn to one of Sandusky's small innovative companies. He took his first job with the Aluminum-Magnesium Company (Al-Mag as its employees called it) as a sales representative.

In the same local tradition of American Crayon's innovation, Al-Mag pioneered the use of lightweight magnesium and aluminum alloys for airplanes during World War II. Founded in the 1930s by Jack Frost, he had followed in the footsteps of Sandusky's innovators. Aluminum was a relatively new metal, strong and light. Frost's use of aluminum had coincidentally flowed out of inventor Charles Martin Hall's experiments in nearby Oberlin, Ohio, in 1886. Hall perfected an inexpensive method for producing the lightweight metal.

The company had grown during World War II by selling airplanes to the government. With the postwar return to consumer goods, Al-Mag supplied the big auto companies, medium-sized manufacturers like Briggs and Stratton and small machine companies. In 1976, Vulcan Materials Company, a Fortune 500 company headquartered in Birmingham, Alabama, acquired Al-Mag and integrated into its metals division.

On the tour, my father introduced me to one of the foremen, Mr. Cooper, an African American man massively built like a defensive end. Mr. Cooper was overseeing a pour of molten aluminum into ingot molds. Like the Roman god Vulcan, he controlled the fire in the furnaces. The flames transformed mixed metals into pure alloys.

I focused on the fire in the furnaces. Fire was also the same force that had started the seed of American Crayon, going back to the fire that cooked up the first batch of chalk at Curtis's kitchen stove. At the first factory, fire beneath vats of hot oil and wax heated and transformed the mixture. Pigments were mixed in, and the hot cylinders were sluiced onto wooden drying racks, where they were dried and cut into crayon segments. Fire had also destroyed American Crayon's first factory. Fire at Vulcan was good; it meant productivity.

My first day of work, I drove to the plant in my summer work car, a 1971 Dodge Dart, lime green with a white vinyl top, bought for $150. Such a car only added to my sour mood. Perhaps the color was an unfortunate evolution of Walter Chrysler's visit to American Crayon in the 1920s, which inspired him to add color to his cars.

My coworker was also summer help and the son of the plant manager. Rail thin, with glasses, he stayed well within the rules, never even hinting that it was possible to have fun. He thought we should ask before we undertook any task or drove somewhere in the company truck to buy supplies. Our job was to clean machines and metal buildings with wire brushes and paint the machinery and buildings. We wore overalls, steel-toed boots, and heavy canvas gloves. Whenever we had to drive the company truck to get more paint or supplies, I made sure I got the keys first and then drove fast and braked hard to raise his level of anxiety for my own entertainment. Because I was bored, I looked for excuses to drive one of the company's pickup trucks to buy supplies. On a couple of the supply runs I would even drive by the crayon company on Hayes Avenue to check up on it. It looked old and worn out with fewer cars in the parking lot.

■◆■◆■◆■

At the end of that summer working at Vulcan Materials, I had scraped and painted machinery and tool sheds and had worked off my sour mood, ready to return for my sophomore year. I sold the lime green Dodge Dart for $150, the same price as I paid for it.

Less than four years later, Vulcan Materials ended production at the plant, laying off 120 workers. The land was sold, the structures were demolished, and the land bulldozed over. The site later reopened as a boat marina that catered to Sandusky's growing demand for summer boaters. Aesthetically and environmentally, it made sense to replace a metals foundry with a boat marina. Like the American Crayon Company had been for my grandfather, Vulcan Materials had been a factory that had given my father his start and twenty-eight years of employment and me, a summer job. And like the American Crayon Company, its buildings were disappearing, as was the spirit of innovation that put the company on the map as the Color Capital of the World.

Chapter 8
Carriage Red

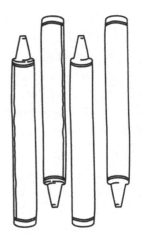

IT WAS SNOWING outside when my mother's Jaguar sports car caught fire in the garage of our house. When the fire department arrived, they quickly smothered the flames using chemical fire extinguishers. The cause of the fire turned out to be a shorted-out electrical system, which plagued her model of Jaguar. My mother's boyfriend, who said he knew about Jaguars, had gone out to start the engine to warm it up and keep it running during the cold weather.

My mother had used money from the sale of inherited Dixon Crucible stock to buy the car, a sleek sports car with V-12 engine, an expensive price tag, and high maintenance costs. Driving the streets of Sandusky, the car stood out among the Detroit-made models like a bird of paradise among a flock of grackles. When my mother would pick me up from middle school football practice, all my teammates would flock to the car. It was a beautiful but flawed car. It had to go to the dealership in Cleveland almost every month to be serviced.

After the fire, the car was declared a total loss by the insurance company and towed away, not to be seen again. At thirteen years old, I assessed the loss in crayon terms. How many boxes of crayons had paid for the car that had melted down into a pile of junk?

By 1973, our family life was falling apart. My father had moved out, and my parents had divorced. A couple of months after the fire, my mother sold our red house on Shady Lane. She decided the house was too much to keep up, and we moved to a series of condominiums in Huron, the next town over.

The day we moved out, my father was there to help us pack and organize the movers. Ann and I sat in my mother's car waiting to leave. With the moving done, my father's last act was to walk down into the unfinished section of the basement and write an inscription in an indelible black marker on the main supporting beam of the house:

> This house built in 1961, by Tom Krammer for Walter and Mary Kropf, daughter Ann born 1959 and son, John born September 1961. Also home to various and sundry dogs and cats, guinea pigs, mice, turtles and a parrot named Hoffman.

The divorce, the move, and the death of my grandmother a few years before made me feel the world was falling apart. We were giving up a house and an intact family. A condominium seemed much less permanent. A condominium seemed the ultimate expression to what had happened to our family.

The outside world in the mid-seventies also seemed to be in decline. TV news was filled with stories of President Nixon's Watergate scandal, the economic shock of the oil crisis of 1973, the US evacuation from Vietnam, and factory layoffs and closings. Sandusky itself seemed to be losing energy. Familiar stores in downtown Sandusky were closing, and land was being cleared south of the town for the new Sandusky Mall.

■◆■◆■◆■

The Whitworths and Curtises had worked with their lawyers to keep as much of the American Crayon stock in the family and set up a trust. The year I was born, the trust unexpectedly came into play. My mother's first cousin, Caroline Whitworth Curtis, died of pneumonia. Caroline had been adopted by my grandfather's older sister, Millie, and her husband. When Caroline died unexpectedly, the stock passed to my mother.

While my mother was pregnant with me, my father called the President of Dixon Crucible to see if he wanted to buy any of the stock, and he asked why my mother was selling. He told him they were a young family with a second child on the way and wanted to buy a house. My father said the president did not ask any more questions and agreed to buy the stock. The windfall was enough for my parents to make a down payment on their first house, a colonial painted Carriage Red, the color chosen by my mother from a collection of Williamsburg Colors sold by the paint company Benjamin Moore. My mother expressed her artistic side by choosing a color that would stand out from the shades of white that predominated the neighborhood. The newly constructed house was built on a tree-lined lane in neighboring Perkins Township, a couple of miles from the original Curtis family farm. Crayons bought the house I came home to.

The year our family moved in, John Kennedy was sworn in as president, Yuri Gagarin became the first man in space, the Berlin Wall was erected, and I came home from Sandusky's Good Samaritan Hospital. Shady Lane had been a long driveway leading to a farm. The farmer had ten acres of land, enough to build an enclave of six houses on either side of the lane, sheltered among a group of mature oaks, maples, and hickory trees. On the eastern side of the lane our back yard ended in a small forest. On the western side of the lane, the backyards emptied into cornfields, and the cornfields rolled on over the horizon, stretching all the way to the farms and prairies of the far Midwest. I felt protected and secure. It was an idyllic place to start a childhood.

■◆■◆■◆■

At thirteen, I tried to confront my mother about what was happening with her money, and she would repeat her phrase, "I was told I never had to worry about money." And so she didn't.

My mother's actions were the opposite of how her father and grand-father would have acted. My great-grandfather had apprenticed in a grocery store and looked for ways to prudently build his wealth. He had studied innovative businesses and what looked like risks to outsiders were carefully considered. He recognized a future in American Crayon. His granddaughter, my mother, had spent money without restraint and resented anyone who told her no. This was partially a product of her time, when women were not encouraged to learn about business, but my mother was smart, and I resented that she didn't recognize the opportunity with an inheritance she could invest and perhaps build something out of what she had received instead of squandering it. She had come from a line of innovators and investors. Instead, we were following a pattern summed up in business school case studies of family businesses—the first generation made the money, the second generation managed, and the third generation spent it.

■◆■◆■◆■

Sandusky's waterfront was a barometer of how the city was doing. It had been a gateway bringing in new settlers starting with the ship pictured on the gold coin, Walk-in-the-Water, and shipped American Crayon products from its port out to the larger world. The company's Kroma division was located down on Water Street in one of the sturdy buildings built from locally sourced limestone.

Sandusky's location on the water had also been a factor in attracting my father to take his first job there. When we drove around town with him, the water was the main entertainment. We would stop at the Jackson Street Pier on Water Street and watch the big freighters pulling into the channel and loading up with coal on the east side of town. Great Lakes freighters, simply called boats by those who worked on them, had distinctive stretched bodies with bridges at the front and superstructure in the back. And in the winter, he would drive to Battery Park, and we would watch the ice boats sail across the frozen bay, moving close to 70 mph as they heeled over on two blades.

To my young imagination, Sandusky's coal docks were like a collection of slow-moving steel monsters. Giant cranes with large scoops that resembled a fifty-foot-tall, metal praying mantis unloaded six-hundred-foot ships. Dark skeletons of steely insects moved slowly and deliberately, dipping into the hold of a ship and scooping out coal for stockpiling.

The other monster was a black, steel tower we called the "coal dumper," nearly one hundred feet high, that looked like a hulking dinosaur skeleton. The inner workings of the coal dumper held a track with a steep incline, like a ski lift, that used a steam-powered push car to push individual train cars, fully loaded with coal, to the top of the ramp. At the top of the incline, the train car would be picked up like it was part of a toy train set, and the contents dumped into the hold of the freighter docked below. Cars could be picked up and dumped at one per minute. The Pennsylvania Railroad found Sandusky's location ideal to bring their coal up from southern Ohio and built three slips that could handle ships up to six hundred feet. By the time my dad and I would watch it, the steam-powered pusher car had already been working tirelessly for the last sixty years. Seen from downtown, photographers used Sandusky's coal docks as a backdrop for orange and red sunsets blossoming at the western end of Sandusky Bay.

With the 1970s slow deterioration, the waterfront also fell into a sad, dilapidated state. The Kroma division of the crayon factory had vacated its space downtown, and the port was no longer used as a place to ship American Crayon products.

■◆■◆■◆■

In November 1975, as I was getting dressed for school, my mother told me that the local radio station, WLEC, had reported that the lake freighter, *Edmund Fitzgerald*, had been lost, with all hands struggling to cross Lake Superior. I was an eighth grader at Huron's McCormack Middle School, and we lived a few blocks from Lake Erie. Outside a nor'easter was wildly shaking the branches of the trees, stripping them of what leaves were still left. The lake churned with white caps and near-gale-force winds.

At the time of the first news report, very little was known about the freighter beyond the fact that it was carrying taconite iron ore pellets from Minnesota's Mesabi range to a steel mill near Detroit. This was scheduled as the ship's final voyage of the season, where it was to move on to Cleveland and tie up for the winter. The *Edmund Fitzgerald* had disappeared from radar in a moment. Maritime experts theorized that the hull likely snapped in half by the immense stress of the waves on the long lines of the ship loaded with thousands of tons of iron ore.

Newsweek magazine reported the tragedy on November 24, 1975, in an article, "The Cruelest Month," reporting November had a long history of ship disasters on the Great Lakes. The story brought national attention to the disaster, surprising the rest of the country, who had little familiarity with the dangers of the inland sea.

Canadian Gordon Lightfoot, a devoted recreational sailor who kept his own boat on the Great Lakes, was among the millions who read the *Newsweek* article, and the next month he wrote and recorded "The Wreck of the Edmund Fitzgerald." The song still has special resonance among the port cities of the Great Lakes, including Sandusky, if not with a generation of people at the time who listened teary-eyed to the news of the devastating loss of dozens of lives in an instant.

■◆■◆■◆■

As soon as I was sixteen, I earned my driver's license and started working as a short-order cook at the fast-food chain, Burger Chef. I used my paychecks to buy a 1970 Pontiac Firebird from a used-car dealer on Sandusky's Perkins Avenue. I had freedom to drive to school and speed along the county's flat county roads.

On the weekends, I liked to drive along Water Street to look at the dark, gritty limestone buildings and factories. As Sandusky grew in the second half of the 1800s, its builders realized the native limestone deposits made a ready resource for construction of houses, schools, factories, a courthouse, and churches between the 1850s until the early twentieth century. Limestone was often quarried near the building site. Quarries were opened around Sandusky, Marblehead, Johnson's Island, and Kelly's Island. They could withstand the hard winters and had a cooling effect in the hot summers. When I was a child, they seemed like castles with their massive stone walls. The buildings still stood as skeletons of their grand past, but most had lost their business and were shuttered.

Driving the streets, I was reminded of my grandmother, the history detective standing in front of her wall of people and places connected by crisscrossing lines of connection to one another. I began to visualize her stories with my drive downtown as if there were a giant ball of string attached from one building to another—from the building on Water Street where Kroma colors were made, around the block along Columbus Avenue to the Whitworth Building, and then along Hayes Avenue to connect to the house where my great-grandparents were married, which happened to be a house on the Underground Railroad. Strings could run back and forth connecting to the Follett house and the abolitionist homes of Sloane and Root. I could see the history of the town, American Crayon, and my family as a vast network of intersecting strings.

Circling the downtown blocks, I also drove by the State Theater and the Ohio Theater where Ann and I had seen *Snow White and the Seven Dwarfs*, *Bambi*, and so many other children's movies. Their marquees were dark. The State Theater showed fewer movies and eventually stopped showing movies altogether. By the time I was a teenager, the Ohio Theater had started showing adult X-rated movies. My sister even called the theater owner to tell him he should be ashamed of himself. To me it was a symbol that something was wrong with Sandusky. When the Sandusky Mall opened, there was a multiplex cinema there, which essentially pushed the downtown theaters to darken their screens. The mall was where high school students would go meet, hang out, and walk around.

In the 1960s, most families shopped in downtown Sandusky. Columbus Avenue had LaSalle's Department Store, a small northern Ohio chain of stores. There was a women's clothing boutique, Carol Crane, with her tagline, "Sandusky's first lady of fashion." My mother would shop for clothes with Ann and me and while she tried on dresses. Ann had us strike different poses with the mannequins in the store window. My mother was eventually asked to leave "with the children." My father bought his suits down the street at the men's clothing store, Marv Buyer. We bought our school shoes at Flippen's Junior Boot Shop, located in the fortress-like old Masonic building. Those businesses were quickly disappearing.

On weekends, my high school friends and I would drive downtown, restless and looking for something to do. With the businesses closing up, we would explore derelict buildings. We found the building for the now-defunct Lyman Boat Works—a long, cavernous structure on Water Street that had been a mainstay Sandusky-based boat builder. Inside were remains of boat molds, tools, leftover boat parts, and material. In the early 1970s, Lyman Boats had switched from building wooden boats to building fiberglass boats. The switch did not last long, and Lyman soon closed its doors on its production. Exploring the boat works, we found discarded cans of marine paint and boat resin lying around at the far end of the building. One of my friends had sneaked his father's Smith and Wesson .357 magnum out of his house, and we lined up the cans and took turns taking target practice. The shots echoed inside the metal walls as the cans exploded, splattering color all over the walls. The more we shot, the more the noise reverberated off the ceiling, and the more color splattered the walls. It felt like we were in some psychedelic shooting gallery. Shooting at the cans of color gave a quick sensory thrill, but I quickly felt a sense of shame after it was over. It felt as if I was kicking an old friend. Sandusky's Color Capitol status had fallen into a hole, and I was helping dig its grave.

Chapter 9
No. 2 Yellow Pencil

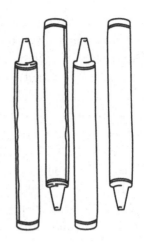

BY THE 1980S, the once state-of-the-art American Crayon factory was well past its prime. It was still using molds and other equipment that had been custom-made, dating back to 1904. The manufacturers of the equipment had long since gone out of business. If machinery broke, replacement parts often had to be custom-made in the factory's maintenance shop. The maintenance staff became critical to keeping the factory running. Old-timers had to transfer knowledge to new staff so they could understand how the intricate machinery operated and how to fix it. Certain staff took on specialties with the factory's machine shop, which served as critical center for constant repairs.

One of the longtime maintenance men, Irvin Baker, mastered the machines that made the chalk pencils.[1] Irvin passed on his stories to his grandson, Ben Baker. The pencils started as cylinders of chalk with layers of paper wrapped around it. A thin string ran along the chalk to tear the paper along a finely perforated edge, exposing a small edge of chalk. The machinery for this was intricately balanced with delicate moving parts. Baker studied the machines and their quirks and learned how they worked. If the chalk machine operator reported something amiss—not enough string measured out, or the paper crooked, or the chalk too short—Baker knew how to adjust it and get the operation back to normal.

The factory building itself was aging. Forklifts, which did not exist when the factory was built, carried heavy pallets of color products. The floor sagged and, in some places, wore through. The maintenance department bolted over the weak spots with large steel plates they called "diamond plates." Thousands of feet of pipe wrapped in 1904-era fire-retardant asbestos had to be carefully painted over every year to contain the dangerous material.

The factory was powered by a coal-fired boiler. The fueling process had become hazardous for the maintenance men who had to climb a ladder up to the coal elevator perched on stilts above the boiler room to service the boiler.

Ben Irvin recalled one of his grandfather's stories in which the plant engineer, Russ Herner, had a preference for a distinct shade of light green and required that any equipment coming into the factory be painted that shade. Through his grandfather, Ben had received one of the cast-off drill presses painted that particular shade of green and continued to use it in his own shop.

During the years Ben's grandfather worked at American Crayon, the factory kept on producing, wearing itself to a nub without new equipment. Irvin's fellow workers developed an admiration for the machine shop's ability to keep the old equipment operating while patching the place together with "spit and chicken wire."

Throughout the 1960s, 1970s, and until the end, American Crayon still held up its reputation of being a family company. Baker's daughter worked on the second floor of the main factory building, running the packaging machines by feeding handfuls of each color crayons into a hopper that fed them down into packaging boxes. Baker's son, Ed, worked for years in what was called the "lead plant," where No. 2 Yellow graphite pencils were made under the Dixon Ticonderoga brand. Baker's son, Steve, worked in the receiving department.

■◆■◆■◆■

The crayons had a magic about them that consistently energized family memories, not just mine. Ben Baker, who recalled his own stories about the factory told many times by his grandfather, mother, and uncles. Ben's grandfather talked so often about the men in the maintenance department he could recite their names by heart: "Vince, Mooch, Henry, the foreman John Camella, became as familiar to me as old friends, though I had never met them." Like me, he enjoyed a bounty of free crayons, paints, or chalk as a kid.

Among his most vivid memories of his grandfather, Ben Baker remembers the sight of his grandfather's hands as he sat at the supper table, "the lines in them blackened with grease and grime that not even Lava soap could wash out. It would be a good while after his retirement that the last of those dark lines finally faded away." It seemed somehow symbolic that the factory had literally gotten into his grandfather's skin.

As the factory grew older, it seemed to shed artifacts as if it were aware of its age and sought to leave behind evidence of itself. The American Crayon employees seemed to understand this. When equipment was replaced or worn out, Irvin Baker would bring home electric motors, an antique air compressor, old hardwood filing cabinets, a 1930s-era Royal typewriter, finger-jointed wooden boxes, and industrial light fixtures. Irvin even brought home brass shavings from the machine shop lathes, copper wiring, and pipe.

In 1984, Bryn Mawr Corporation merged with American Crayon's parent company, Joseph Dixon Crucible, to form Dixon Ticonderoga. The new company began a series of negotiations meant to reassure American Crayon's workers that the Sandusky plant would continue to operate.

A decade later, under President Clinton, the North American Free Trade Agreement (NAFTA) went into effect between the United States, Canada, and Mexico. These reduced labor and trade barriers gave the US access to less expensive labor.

Despite the outdated facility, the plant manager, Jim Alexander, told the *Toledo Blade* he believed they had made the highest-quality product. But the age of the factory with its coal-powered heat had become very expensive and required a lot of maintenance. Without any upgrade to the factory or the machinery, the decision to close must have been apparent even to the maintenance men.

Roger Bibler, a shipping and receiving clerk and president of the union local representing the workers, said the factory was closing because of the greed of management taking advantage of NAFTA. Local civic leaders lobbied Dixon Ticonderoga to apply for Ohio air-quality incentives to install gas heat instead of coal, but Dixon had made its decision.

Irvin Baker formally retired in 1994 but continued on as a consultant. His knowledge of the old machines had been vital to keeping them working, but now he was in the business of knowledge transfer. Dixon Ticonderoga made the decision to move machinery to Canada and Mexico. Management brought some of the Mexican workers to the Sandusky factory and asked if the Sandusky workers would train their replacements, but most refused. Baker was one of the few who saw it through to instruct the new operators about the care and feeding of the old machinery.

The day the factory ceased production, Roger Bibler said in a 2018 interview, "Our oldest man walked out of there after fifty-one or fifty-two years, and cried like a baby." According to Bibler, he never purchased another Dixon Ticonderoga pencil after that day.

Eventually, all the operations were progressively moved out of the Sandusky factory. When the last old machines were moved to a facility in Mexico in 1997, Baker retired for good.

In its official history, Dixon Ticonderoga marked 1995 as the 160th anniversary of American Crayon and the eightieth anniversary of the Old Faithful trademark, but there was no celebration in Sandusky.[2] In 2002, the Hayes Avenue factory officially closed its doors, 130 years after William Curtis started baking chalk in the family oven. American Crayon had once been the largest and oldest employer in Sandusky.

The closing of the crayon factory was also felt at the Station House, a restaurant and bar across the street. Sally Bagley, a cook for thirty-five years at the restaurant known for decades as Ev's Corner, told the local press, "I'm going to say it'll be hard on us."[3] The restaurant had been filled at capacity with the plant employees, but its regulars had dwindled to about half a dozen workers for lunch.

The relocated factory in Mexico later went bankrupt. I imagine that the intricate machinery had given its final effort, but that the move a thousand miles south was too much for it. Perhaps there was some small irony at work on the equipment from the American Crayon Company. It was not meant to operate anywhere else but Sandusky, Ohio, USA.

■◆■◆■◆■

Over the years, Sandusky would occasionally be the punch line for jokes. We did not get the brunt of them like our older sibling Cleveland and its legacy of the Burning River and "the mistake on the lake," but I thought the city got more than its share, considering its modest size. In 1980, *National Lampoon* editor and Toledo, Ohio, native P. J. O'Rourke published *The King of Sandusky, Ohio*, a parody of a medieval struggle using Sandusky's blandness as a foil. The next year, an *Omni Magazine* movie review of *Outland*, an outer space movie set on a grim mining colony on one of Jupiter's moons, described the setting as "dismal as Sandusky, Ohio." My first thought was I wanted to punch this wise-guy reviewer in the nose.

I knew Sandusky had none of the quaintness of the New England town common or the luxurious, sunny climate of Southern California. Yes, it carried a raw and pallid three-season grayness of any small-sized Midwestern industrial town, but I knew we still carried the title Color Capital of the World. The hard part was that no one in the present world remembered the distinction. I was not certain the last time anyone used the phrase.

Like-minded citizens, proud of Sandusky's heritage, formed a group in 1983 called Friends of the Boeckling, which financed an effort to rescue the former Sandusky steamship, the *Boeckling* from Sturgeon Bay, Wisconsin, where it had been used as a floating warehouse and machine shop. The community raised money to restore the old ship, but the project ended in disaster when the *Boeckling* was destroyed by a fire as she sat at a mooring in Toledo's Maumee River in 1989. Arson was suspected in the early morning fire.[4] Somehow it seemed sadly symbolic for the difficult time Sandusky had entered. A core of history-minded Sanduskians had sought to save the city's past, but their good intentions met with a tragic end.

■◆■◆■◆■

More Sandusky companies closed their doors. After American Crayon, one of the city's oldest employers, Hinde and Dauch Paper Company, ceased operations in Sandusky in 1981. Nearby Scott Paper Company, which made paper towels and toilet paper, closed its factory in 1980. Scott Paper had sponsored an academic high school competition for Erie County called Hi-Q (I was on the team for Huron High School). The west end of Sandusky's waterfront had become a grimy collection of shuttered factories, warehouses, and crumbling docks. The Sandusky Foundry and Machine Company, the only remaining foundry, still operated at a reduced size for a parent company in Wisconsin making specialized metal alloys.

Ferrell-Cheek Steel Company closed in 1983 after seventy-three years of operation. Barr Rubber Products, which had returned to making recreational balls and toys and rubber components for boats and automobiles after World War II, suffered. The factory closed in 1986 due to declining sales. The closures were miniature versions of what our big siblings of Pittsburgh, Cleveland, and Detroit were undergoing.

At about the same time, the metals company, Vulcan Materials, where my father had first worked and where I had a summer job, closed its operations, and the buildings were demolished.

The neglected Ohio Theater downtown was razed in 1985. Two blocks away, the State Theater, which had endured a period of neglect, escaped the wrecking ball and was saved by being placed on the National Register of Historic Places in 1988.

■◆■◆■◆■

History describes many gateways that explorers pass through on their way out to the wider unknown world. Gateways mark the beginning of a quest to overcome doubts or achieve some greater understanding. For the Greeks, it was the Pillars of Hercules at the western end of the Mediterranean, for the Romans it was the Stone Tower somewhere in the Pamirs that was a portal to Asia and the routes of the Silk Road. For the Cowdery-Curtis families, it had been the Great Genesee Road leading them out of New England to find new lives in the Midwest. For me, the Ohio Turnpike Exit 7, smack in the middle of northern Ohio, was my gateway out of Sandusky. The Turnpike had been the long-term replacement to the Lake Shore Electric trains connecting Sandusky to a network of northern Ohio stations connecting Cleveland and Toledo. When I accepted my toll ticket and then had to face the metallic green and white lettered interstate signs with a choice of East to Cleveland or West toward Toledo, I read them as New York or Chicago. The highway would carry me to big cities with department stores, expensive restaurants, and museums. As a kid, I thought of them as important cities, because that's where they had television stations. If there was an advantage to being in between it was that you could receive signals from Cleveland, Toledo, and sometimes Detroit.

Growing up, Exit 7 meant the start of an exciting journey—at least to Cleveland. Exit 7 was a break in the monotony of cornfields, ranch-style motels, and a factory that made asphalt shingles. If I had been a six-year-old designing highways and scenery with crayons and news-print, I would have added more Redwood trees, hairpin curves, tunnels, and purple mountains.

■◆■◆■◆■

1988 was eventful year for me. I graduated from law school, took the bar exam, and moved to Washington, DC, to start my first adult job at the Department of Justice. In the few weeks I had before starting work, I returned to Sandusky to wander the downtown. I mostly drove down around the waterfront and the industrial areas with my oldest child-hood friend, Kirk, without any purpose. It left me with a sense of sadness, and I hoped to see something more exciting before I left town.

Without discussion, we drove past the dark buildings of the crayon factory and Hayes Avenue and toward the waterfront. We parked downtown and stood in the middle of Columbus Avenue facing north toward Sandusky Bay; across the street, the darkened State Theater, and the ferry docks with boats to Cedar Point, the western Lake Erie Islands and Canada. This was still the "land of the cold water," but no longer the Color Capital of the World.

My great-grandfather, the son of an immigrant mechanic, had dem-onstrated his business abilities to the Sandusky merchants to move from grocer to the town's most prominent banker. He then used his business sense to take educated risks, financing new businesses like American Crayon. By comparison, I doubted whether I could have accepted the same risks of leaving my country for the unknown. I was risk averse, planning a safe direction in my career. I moved to Washington, DC, to work as a government attorney in a safe government job. Had I known the chances that my great-grandfather had taken, maybe I would have acted differently. I never considered taking a chance and had not thought about going into what amounted to today's world as a start-up. I realize now that my risk avoidance was more a reaction to my parent's generation.

I thought of the stories of my great-grandfather as distant myths that were not directly connected to me. If I had the fortitude, I would have taken inspiration from my great-grandfather and thought about going into a business and perhaps thinking in more innovative ways. Could I have risked financial stability in lieu of exploring an opportunity? Were there new opportunities in my hometown I should have been looking for? I was haunted by the idea I should be taking risks, but more recent history with my mother's financial recklessness weighed against this. No. I was looking for boring stability.

■◆■◆■◆■

The next day, after exploring Sandusky's downtown, I looked at the small, brick, ranch-style house where my mother was living and all the family artifacts that she had collected, and I wondered if it would all fade away. It was twelve degrees above zero when we drove out to Oakland Cemetery with my mother that day. We walked her two lab mixes to different collections of family gravestones. She repeated stories about the Whitworths, Curtises, and Cowderys and their family gatherings. I wanted to interrupt to say I'd heard them all many times, but I stopped myself. This was important mythology for her to recite among the graves of "her people."

I drove back to Washington, DC, fighting the nagging sensation that I was wasting my life and that I had missed some crucial sign or had not noticed someone important along the way.

■◆■◆■◆■

While I was away living in Washington, DC, Sandusky continued to change. The massive New Departure plant, Erie County's largest employer, was sold off by GM, and over time the new owners laid off hundreds more workers before closing in 2017. Chrysler had sold its plant in 1992. Many of my high school friends' parents had worked at the auto plants, including the father of one of my best friends who worked the New Departure division of General Motors in a high-level engineering position. If someone went to high school in Erie County and wanted to go straight to factory work, it was an easy transition. Sandusky High School students could walk across Perkins Avenue to the GM plant the day after graduation and begin their working lives.

GM, Ford, and Chrysler factories had all operated in Sandusky. This was now the second time the auto companies went away.

■◆■◆■◆■

The Cowderys and Curtises had made Sandusky their home since the 1840s, and the Whitworths since 1855. My great-grandfather started a grocery store, became a bank president, and founded a crayon company. All that had come to an end. My mother was an only child and had done what she could to keep her family name alive one more generation by giving both Ann and me the middle name of Whitworth. And then in 1998, when my mother moved out of Sandusky to Savannah, Georgia, to be near my sister, the family's physical presence in Sandusky ended.

■◆■◆■◆■

Fifteen years after its machinery had been removed, the American Crayon factory sat vacant. The 1902 state-of-the-art building, pride of an inventive Sandusky, became an embarrassing eyesore. There were false starts to tear it down, but the expense of demolishing a building filled with asbestos frustrated companies considering the job. The dilapidated structure was considered a safety hazard that threatened to collapse on the Norfolk and Southern train tracks that ran alongside the factory. The factory lost all its working souls and was left to sit in humiliation, with its distinctive white lettering, "The American Crayon Company Sandusky Ohio," clearly displayed for everyone to see.

In 2013, *The Sandusky Register* ran stories about the slow death of the building, quoting structural experts who gave the factory another

couple of weeks. Two years later, the factory was still standing, collecting more broken windows. Curiosity seekers climbed through holes in
the chain-link fence with snow on the ground and filmed the desic-
cated inside, showed termite damage to the giant supporting beams,
and pulled out bricks from the disintegrating walls. It was like watching
someone poke around the corpse of a deceased friend.[5]

The images could not have been sadder against the bleak northern
Ohio winter sky. Ben Irvin, the grandson who had heard his grandfather's
stories about American Crayon, even though he had moved to New
England, saw the stories too and commented that the "old factory called
to me even more." Coincidentally, he had gone into business crafting and
repurposing old wood. Shortly before the factory was to be torn down,
he got his chance to save some of its bones. The site had been purchased
at foreclosure auction by a Texas-based company specializing in the
teardown of old buildings for salvage. Ben purchased some of the original wood to be repurposed for his handcrafted wood business.

■◆■◆■◆■

Economists call it creative destruction. The destruction of the factory
was nothing new. Other industries came and went. Railroads and
telegraphs destroyed the Pony Express. Automobiles made horse-drawn
carriages obsolete. But didn't everyone need crayons made in the
Midwest? No matter how digital the world became, wouldn't children
still need crayons to illustrate what they saw in their imaginations? The
hopeful answer was yes, but there was more to it than that.

Behind the black brick walls, the factory and its workers brought
new color into the everyday world. The colorful crayons and paints
were the tools for millions of imaginations. Dover white chalk conveyed
the newness of an idea, whether it was presented by nervous elementary school students or Nobel Prize-winning professors. All that creativity and thinking got its start in the factory. How many teachers in
one-room schoolhouses or professors at Ivy League universities had
mapped out their lessons using American Crayon chalk? How many
millions of children drew pictures of sunsets with Prang watercolors
and had their work pinned up by proud parents on the family refrig-

erator? How many art students went on to create their work from using American Crayon tempera paints? How many houses were built using carpenters' chalk, or clothes designed by fashion workers using tailor's chalk? How many first drafts of great literature (and not so great) were written with Sandusky-made pencils? They were instruments of every-day creativity. I wonder if Marcellus Cowdery had foreseen all the ideas expressed on blackboards scripted by the improved chalk. The creativity that flowed from the fingertips of the teachers, artists, and writers through products of the factory was incalculable.

Maybe it is the child in everyone. Crayons have the power to inspire, and having a crayon factory nearby might seem like the closest thing to an eternal fountain of youth. Dozens of comments on Sandusky's history blog express affection, with many posts recounting how the factory was a favorite school field trip. Sandusky residents had snuck behind the chain-link fence erected around the perimeter of the old factory and rescued wooden packing crates, boxes, signs, and even bricks. Some devotees collected their crayons, and one even built a small shrine in his home. Would the teardown of an insurance company building inspire the same compassion for its artifacts of desks and file cabinets?

Can a factory have a soul?

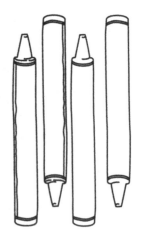

Chapter 10
Orange Trees

EVEN THOUGH I broke the physical ties to Sandusky in 1988 when I moved to Washington, DC, my crayon mythology stayed with me. I suppose it even haunted me. I thought of the two John Whitworths, father and son, and the Pasadena house, the house that crayons built. In Sandusky, the American Crayon factory was operating at diminished capacity with Prang continuing as its strongest brand. The parent company, Dixon Ticonderoga, had moved its headquarters from Jersey City, New Jersey, to Vero Beach, Florida in 1985.

If I could not become a part of American Crayon's enterprise, I would find other ways to connect to the legacy of crayons. I turned to my grandfather and namesake, John Whitworth, to follow in the footsteps of his life before joining the company as an officer. I was about to enter into my own adult job with the US Government.

I had carried my grandfather's logbook from his 1919 cross-country adventure when he got out of the army. The pages of the journal, kept in a black leather three-ring binder, contained black-and-white photographs showing my grandfather and his crew wearing an assortment of World War I–era leather aviator helmets and leggings. The men were cradling rifles, staging snowball fights in northern Arizona, and standing next to a huge monster of an automobile. My favorite photo, taken somewhere on the rise of a dirt road on the eastern plains of Colorado, showed the Fiat with two oversized American flags streaming from the front fenders. At the top of the front grillwork, I could make out the Fiat cloisonné-nameplate. This was the Fiat's "eye." I called it the "Eye of the Cyclops" and for me, it is the most powerful crayon artifact, though its luminous color was lost in the black-and-white photograph.

At twenty-six, my last year of law school, and the same age as my grandfather when he made his drive, I decided to take a trip in John's footsteps to the fabled house. Maybe it would help me know the unknown grandfather and learn about my own identity. During those Sunday night dinners at my grandmother's house, I had driven my toy cars along the Whitworth's oriental carpets on the floor in her family room. My grandfather had an urge to drive across the country, and so did I.

The idea for the trip came to me while I was sitting in my Wills, Trusts, and Estates class during my last year of law school while staring at the blood-red case book. I had put off this required class until the end of my law school curriculum. My pattern was to plot the safe course, but the trip would be my allotment of freedom like a prisoner out on parole.

The route would be the same: Sandusky to Pasadena. If nothing else, I figured I could at least see the same sky and landscape John had seen.

■◆■◆■◆■

Cars were in the family blood. As a teenager, my grandfather became an early adopter. In 1912, American Crayon money had allowed him at the age of seventeen to buy a Willys Overland, one of the first four-wheel-drive cars manufactured by a new company in nearby Toledo, and precursor to millions of today's SUVs (Willys Overland later made the Jeep for the military during World War II.) The Willys was his classroom. After driving on the muddy farm roads around Erie County, he would park it behind the family house on Hayes Avenue in Sandusky, dismantle the engine, and rebuild it. His fascination with innovative technology would later guide his future.

While American Crayon was adapting to business during the war, my grandfather left his sophomore year at Caltech to enlist in the army. In December 1917, he applied at the Los Angeles army recruiting office but was initially rejected for unspecified reasons. I imagined that this small, quiet man from a family of privilege had some internal sense of duty and was determined to follow his sense of duty to his country. My mother said he was the only one of his cousins to enlist. Two days before Christmas, to the distress of his mother and sisters, he took a train to arrive at the cold, damp climate of Angel's Island in San Francisco Bay. He stood with the volunteers in formation outside in the Pacific fog and mist for ten hours and was finally enlisted.

Because my grandfather loved cars, he requested duty in the motor pool. By the time he was shipped to boot camp at Camp Arthur Texas, my grandfather showed flu-like symptoms, and army doctors misdiagnosed him with tuberculosis, which was then nearly an epidemic in the country. The doctors were firm in their diagnosis and even sent a Western Union telegram to his mother saying only "YOUR SON JOHN CRITICAL CONDITION. COME IMMEDIATELY." He was to be transferred and confined to an army TB sanatorium, where he was nearly certain to catch the highly contagious disease that he did not have. Through the persistence of his mother, Carrie Whitworth, private doctors, and a powerful family member, Judge Price, a Kansas state senator, the diagnosis was corrected, and my grandfather avoided the sanatorium and was properly treated for pneumonia. Erie County had lost a total of fifty-six soldiers during the war, almost half of them due to the waves of TB and influenza that had swept the country.

In July 1918, my grandfather was honorably discharged and warned by the army doctors that he should not expect to father children. He returned to Pasadena to regain his health. My grandfather never fulfilled his wish to serve his country in the Great War.

During my grandfather's recovery, he had time to think. He was determined to achieve some sense of personal accomplishment since he had not gone to war. He devised his own adventure to travel to his parents' Pasadena house from Sandusky, across the country, by car.

I guessed that my grandfather may have formulated his idea during one of his many train trips west from Sandusky. He may have also read about a trip that had taken place a few months earlier led by a young army Colonel, Dwight Eisenhower, in charge of the first-ever army convoy from Washington, DC, to California. Colonel Eisenhower was leading men to do what my grandfather had signed up to do.

He probably used his crayon inheritance from his father to buy a car suitable for the adventure. After the near-death ordeal with the army's doctors, it would be hard to imagine his family would have denied the only Whitworth son this adventure. The car he selected from the Carlton-Shepard-Bowles distributors in Los Angeles was an exotic, monster-sized Fiat Riviera Type 56. The Fiat sales brochure described the car as the product of one of the first American automobile joint ventures, built as part of Italian American collaboration in Poughkeepsie, New York.

The Fiat was not a cheap car, with a price tag close to $6,000 (about $90,000 in 2020). It was intended to compete with American prestige cars at the time, such as the Thomas Peerless, Lozier, and the Pierce-Arrow.

My grandfather convinced cousin Earl and two Sandusky friends to join him in the adventure: Henry Harbrecht, Harry Beilstein, and briefly, cousin Lynn Curtis, who returned by train once they reached Indianapolis. Earl and John had been close since their earliest days growing up next door to each other. Twenty years earlier, they drove a pony cart together down Hayes Avenue, and it was not hard to imagine they were still boys playing around. The thirty-one-year-old Earl was married with a five-year-old daughter. The decade before, he had started as an office boy at American Crayon and learned the business from the factory's operations as an office manager and purchasing agent. John and Earl had family in Pasadena. Henry, a friend of my grandfather's since high school who shared an interest in early automobiles, held a stake in the Hinde and Dauch Paper Company, another of Sandusky's innovative enterprises. He had a spirit of adventure and planned to see his mother and sister in Southern California. Harry had no family in California but hoped to visit relatives along the way in Arizona.

On Tuesday, November 4, 1919, the crew assembled in front of Sandusky's main post office. It happened to be Election Day, and *The Sandusky Register* reported that the vote on the Versailles Peace Treaty was still in deadlock in the Senate and an issue was on the Erie County ballot to approve two million dollars for a Good Roads levy, which would pass by a wide margin. Sandusky's incumbent mayor would be defeated that day. The county's citizens also voted to repeal Ohio's state law on prohibition, not surprising because of all the breweries and wineries in the region.

Under gray clouds and threatening rain, John took a picture looking down Columbus Avenue to Sandusky Bay on the day of the crew's departure. A lake steamer is clearly seen at the dock with black smoke wafting from its smokestack.

John pulled the Fiat out into Columbus Avenue and turned south on Hayes Avenue, the same road Charles Dickens had traveled going north to Sandusky by stagecoach almost eighty years earlier.

The crew's mechanical skills kept the car going, driving the thousands of miles of mud roads and wagon trails, getting stuck in ditches, fighting "gumbo mud" and battery fires, changing endless flat tires, and sleeping in haystacks. At a blacksmith's shop in Missouri, they had to custom-smelt a bearing to replace one in the car that had seized up.

As they drove, my grandfather's thoughts about the crayon business were never far away. Crossing the prairie of southwestern Kansas, in Ashland, population 1,100, the crew stopped at the town's Main Street drugstore with a soda fountain run by an elderly lady. My grandfather was so heartened by the family's products, he noted in the logbook "saw an American Crayon product, 30 Blendwell & Kroma school paints... it seems good to run into something from Sandy."

After a total of thirty days of arduous travel, the crew approached Pasadena. My grandfather made the following entry in his logbook: "Twenty miles east of Pasadena, the Last leg of the trip. J. C. W. driver. Rain."

Mother Nature relented and granted the crew a small reward for the end of the Trail. The next entry: "PASADENA. One hour and fifty-five minutes from San Bernardino. Sun coming out. TOTAL MILEAGE 2676."

Pasadena had been the end of the trip for my grandfather. The crayon prosperity allowed my great-grandfather to build an arts-and-crafts-style winter retreat, complete with a small orange grove, something my grandfather relished seeing. He had driven from Sandusky's gray skies to Pasadena's green palm trees with Cousin Earl and his friends to arrive at the place that was his second home. Perhaps the journey was some sort of redemption for the war he did not fight with his comrades. He was now home. The Pasadena house meant shelter, food, and a place to rest. More importantly, the Pasadena home meant he would be with his mother and sister.

■◆■◆■◆■

Seventy years after my grandfather's journey, I retraced his trip, keeping my own logbook in an identical style. The passing miles brought to light comparisons and contrasts between the parallel journeys. It took my grandfather thirty days to travel the country. The Fiat averaged 25 mph and fifty miles on a good day. There were no marked roads, no fellow travelers, and no help available in case of trouble. By contrast, I could have crossed the country in three days on four-lane interstates, but I insisted on following the smaller county roads as close to the original route as possible.

I retraced the route but didn't see any American Crayon products in Ashland, Kansas, or anywhere else along the way. I arrived at the Whitworth house in Pasadena at the time of the day photographers call the "golden hour." The house's distinctive features matched up with the black-and-white pictures: whitewashed stucco walls, the double L-shaped wings that pointed toward the street, the main entrance with its curved walkway. The grass looked brown and slightly worn and in need of some attention. Tall palm trees and desert plants flanked both sides of the house, giving it a slightly exotic feel. Two large, burnt-orange vases, about four feet high, sat at either side of the entrance. Potted in each were large, bushy shrubs.

The family house was now a halfway shelter for adults recovering from alcohol and drug addictions named Hope Manor. I accepted a tour inside from the shelter's director on duty. It was as if the structure emanated a genealogical force field that pulled me across the country. The house had been saturated with the words, emotions, and spirits of three generations of my ancestors unknown to me. I described the irrational sense of entitlement I felt as "the clan instinct"—wanting to possess something for no other reason than that your ancestors had once owned it.

Our guide led us outside into the back courtyard. I hurried to take a few pictures as the shadows stretched out behind the house. I had to remember to look for a small grove of orange trees. They were the one detail that my grandmother included in every story about the house. The director was surprised when I asked about the orange grove. The trees were still there in the shadows of the back yard.

The visit was like watching a 3-D movie of a favorite book. I imagined myself at this very spot as if I had stepped through a photograph taken the day my grandfather arrived after his long journey. I could picture a scene with the mud-splattered Fiat driving into the courtyard carrying the road-weary crew. I focused my senses on what may grandfather would have known: the smell of the orange grove, the feel of the mahogany wood trim of the doorways, the view of the intricate brick design of the courtyard. The Pasadena house was no longer a faded photograph in an album or a story from my grandmother's dinner table.

The next morning, after imposing myself on a friend of a friend who lived in the Hollywood Hills and sleeping on the floor of her house, I pointed my car east. I had completed my pilgrimage, following my grandfather's tire tracks. Like my grandfather, obligations awaited with a new job and the world of adulthood. The return trip would be interstate all the way back to the East Coast—"John driving."

■◆■◆■◆■

My grandfather had the Fiat shipped back to Sandusky by a flatbed freight car, while he returned by train. There is no account of his return trip, probably because train travel was considered routine. The decision to return by train is not hard to imagine. It would have been like deciding to cross the North Atlantic in a square-rigger when a White Star ocean liner was available—round trip. The thirty-day trek from Ohio to California had shown that in 1919, a cross-country automobile drive was still more an adventure than a practical way to travel. A return drive might have exceeded the mechanical and mental limits of the car and crew.

What happened to the Fiat when it returned to Sandusky is unclear. The one piece of the car that came down to me was the oval Fiat name-plate that was attached at the top of the grill. I imagined my grandfather must have pried it off of the car before he parted ways with the great machine.

When he returned, my grandfather began his career in the family business at American Crayon Company and lived in Sandusky the remainder of his life. By 1948, he could no longer afford to maintain a house in California and live and work in Ohio. The house that symbolized his father's dreams, earned with crayon money, was sold.

■◆■◆■◆■

Like my grandfather, my pilgrimage to Pasadena was a slice of freedom of the open road before joining the working world. For him, joining the family Color Capital company was his next step. For me, it was starting as a first-year attorney at the Department of Justice.

I thought of my own future without the crayon myths and the future of cross-country travel and wondered if future generations would embark on their own journeys of discovery. Before I met my wife Eileen and before my daughter Charlotte was born, I speculated whether I might have a grandchild who would retrace John Whitworth's route, my route, and add even more miles to the trail. It seemed fitting that in America, land of the automobile, generations unknown to each other could form an ancestral bond driving across the country. If there was one connection from the three-thousand-mile drive, it was that John had passed on something more than crayons and a logbook. He had passed on the need to have a hero's journey.

The Pasadena house was built from the prosperity of the crayon factory in Sandusky. My great-grandfather had never enjoyed the benefit of what he had created from the world of color. He was part of the family that created the Color Capital of the World under the gray skies of northern Ohio and had a dream that he would relax in the warm desert world of Southern California with its colorful orange groves and sunsets.

To me, Southern California history felt foreign. The cold water of my native Sandusky heightened the contrast. Three generations before me, the Whitworth family put down roots here, but they did not last. Southern California was something that shouldn't belong to the cold and gray of the Midwest. I might have taken a cross-country journey had there never been a Pasadena house, but I wouldn't have taken *this* journey.

I suppose if I had been born a generation earlier, I would have stayed in Sandusky and focused on the manufacturing of crayons. Instead, I moved back east, reversing the course of my ancestors from three generations before. I looked to the security of employment in Washington, DC, and later, without intending to, stayed to work in the information age. When I started my professional life in 1988, I felt I could finally set aside the idea of Sandusky's Color Capital legacy.

Later that year, when I had to explain to my insurance company why I had clocked such a high number of miles on my car in the first year, the agent quipped over the phone, "You drove all the way across the country for a pack of crayons?"

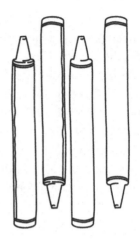

Chapter 11
Paper District Imperial
Brown Ale

LIVING IN ARLINGTON, Virginia, the American Crayon Company's colorful heritage had faded from my memory and, instead, I noticed random references over the years that had transformed Sandusky into a joke for Hollywood. The 1995 comedy, *Tommy Boy,* showed Tommy Callahan III (Chris Farley) as a good-natured but dopey heir to Callahan Auto, a factory in Sandusky that manufactured auto parts. After barely graduating from college, Tommy returns to Sandusky but continues his goofball behavior, somehow saving Callahan Auto from going under.

Like the American Crayon Company, the rest of Sandusky had lost its industrial edge. The innovative generations that Cowdery-Curtis had been a part of since the 1860s had persevered all the way through the Great Depression and World War II. After the War, Erie County had seemed to slip into complacency, relying on the revenues of the big automobile plants that had come in, but they were not local innovators. Sandusky was used as a convenient and inexpensive location for each industry's supply chain. When the crayon factory and other plants shut down, the revenues declined. After the city reached its high-water mark of 32,000 people in 1970, residents continued to move away from the city. By 2000, the city had shrunk to 28,000 residents and was on a downward slide.[1]

In 2009, Sandusky resident John Hamilton was arrested for mowing unkempt grass in the city's Central Park. He told *The Sandusky Register* that he simply wanted to make his city look nice.[2] Police said they arrested Hamilton after he refused to stop mowing and charged him with obstructing official business and disorderly conduct. After the story gained national attention as a symbol of an anemic local government, one national commentator wrote, "Sandusky... can go straight to Hell." The charges against Hamilton, who was dubbed by the media as "the lawnmower man," were dropped, and that November he was elected to the Sandusky City Commission.

■◆■◆■◆■

In 2015, the year after I ordered American Crayons on eBay, adult coloring books were selling out all over the country, with an estimated twelve million coloring books sold that year, up from eleven million in 2014.[3] August 2, 2015, was designated as the first National Coloring Book Day. Crayon clubs and collecting blogs appeared on social media. Perhaps the most thorough of the sites, CrayonCollecting.com, was maintained by collector Ed Welter. Crayons seemed to be fulfilling some basic adult enjoyment. I wondered what the old Sandusky school master Marcellus Cowdery would have thought about the craze. Once again, a small part of me stirred and wished American Crayon had survived to supply the crayons for the surge in adult artists. Instead, the crayon factory was crumbling down, waiting for the demolition company's wrecking ball.

■◆■◆■◆■

That same year, my sister Ann died from cancer. I returned to Sandusky to bury her, bringing with me our family crayon stories. My route was a long one—a drive from Arlington, Virginia, to Sandusky by way of Savannah, Georgia, where Ann had raised a family for twenty-three years. Ann and my mother had lived in the same house.

In addition to collecting my sister's ashes, I had to move my mother into a nursing home and sort through her belongings. My mother was the last Whitworth, and what was left of the crayon relics funneled down to me. I dubbed them "crayon artifacts." They had made their own journeys, being collected, sorted, broken up, and moved for more than 120 years to different households. The crayon artifacts reminded me of a snowball rolling down a mountain in the hot sun.

When I arrived at my sister's small, ranch-style house to move my mother and start my sort, I made a pile for smaller items that would fit in my station wagon for the drive back to Arlington. I made a second pile of larger items that would need to go into storage. My dilemma was deciding what I should keep and what should be moved on. Our Arlington house was small, with too much furniture and too many books. I debated with myself whether to haul it all to charity rather than having the headache of paying for the storage or moving it. But I was paying to move the stories attached to them—objects associated with people in my history. I could not think of it as *just stuff*. It was as if I was the last archaeologist who understood this civilization of people, and I needed to preserve their artifacts for further study to share with the rest of the world. The downside was that these were objects carted around generation after generation, like a horse pulling a cart that has more and more weight added to it as the journey moves along. During the sort, I came across some of the penny stock certificates I had seen in our garage when I was nine.

In my mother's top dresser drawer, I found a brown leather Marc Cross case that belonged to my grandfather. The case still had the suppleness of a well-used baseball mitt, even after seventy years. The case held his cuff links and a gold deputy sheriff's badge for Erie County that had "J. C. Whitworth" inscribed at the top. As a kid, my mother would let me pin the gold badge on my shirt and play sheriff with neighborhood friends, never knowing the history behind it.

An unlikely possession of my mother's was a blue, red, and gold cloisonné Fiat oval shaped nameplate that had been mounted at the top of my grandfather's 1915 Fiat. The nameplate was like a small shield and displayed the word "Fiat" in an art deco design. It was worthy of being worn as jewelry, but it had pointed the giant car west, its crew driving dirt trails through the elements of sun, dust, rain, and snow. The marker was the only remnant of the giant car and it had seen the gumbo mud of Missouri and the mesas of New Mexico coming to rest in the brick courtyard of the Pasadena house, shaded by a grove of California orange trees. Perhaps my grandfather needed to retain some reminder of the car when he pried it out of the inset above the radiator grill and set it aside in his top dresser drawer. When I sold my VW Jetta, the car I drove to retrace his trail, it would not have been worth prying the chrome-colored plastic VW from the grillwork, but I did keep the Virginia license plates together with the owner's manual.

The vestiges of my grandfather's mechanical abilities remained in my backyard garden shed in Arlington in the form of his oak cabinet-maker's workbench filled with some of his original tools. The bench was handed down to me by my father, who had received it from my grandmother. I remember that it sat in the corner of our basement in our family house, and many Saturdays my father actively used the metal vice to fix, mend, or paint some small household project. The bench had three stacked drawers with a raised wood panel at the back filled with holes to hold screwdrivers and an assortment of other tools.

I had pieces of his car, the aroma of his tobacco, his personal shaving kit, his writings, and even a wooden shipping crate from the factory stenciled "American Crayon Company, Sandusky, Ohio." All of it flowed from the prosperity of the company. Through the wealth of stories and the possessions, I thought I could know the man by touching and retracing his experience.

During the drive with Ann's ashes and the cargo, I thought of how the crayon artifacts came from the crayon factory's prosperity. But I wondered what happened to the innovation and wealth that came with it? Why didn't it continue? Why couldn't I be working in the business of crayons where I watch color being made?

The heirlooms flowed from the "crayon money" and were reminders of the Curtis inventiveness and the Whitworth risk-taking. Hot vats of wax were mixed with hundreds of varieties of pigments, poured into molds, and transformed into colorful crayons. Ironically, there was not a single crayon among the carload of artifacts.

That June I returned to Sandusky with my father, Ann's three children, Mary Ann, Olivia, and Daniel, to inter Ann's cremated remains at Oakland Cemetery. The morning of Ann's internment, I collected my father and Ann's children from our motel outside of Sandusky and drove the five of us with Ann's urn to the cemetery. Our approach to the cemetery traveled along Milan Road, State Route 250, the road Ann and I had traveled hundreds of times. This had once been a two-lane road but had been widened to four lanes and lined with miles of big box stores and the full array of fast-food restaurants.

We slowed down on Milan Road to make the turn into Oakland Cemetery and drove past graceful black iron gates hinged on granite columns that were swung shut and locked at night. The Moore sisters' granite book gravestone was an immediate reminder of Ann's love of books and the Cowdery legacy.

Inside the cemetery's iron gates, we pulled into a narrow grass lane into what my mother called "the old section" under the shade of century-old oaks and parked alongside the family headstone. There was a Whitworth family plot that had been purchased and first used for my great-grandfather and great-grandmother and then later my mother's parents. Now we had skipped a generation and were interring Ann.

Still in Savannah, my mother was under hospice care, confined to a bed in a nursing home and unable to make the trip. When the time came, my mother had said she wanted to be cremated and interred alongside her parents in Oakland. From her bed, she talked frequently of her parents' large home on Sandusky's Wayne Street and the Whitworth house in Pasadena, California.

I thought about all those stately homes and properties and how I might have inherited a house or land. There were no homes left and the last land that passed down to me through my great-grandfather, John Whitworth, was a cemetery family plot. I had inherited enough land for two full body burials.

Our minimalist burial of Ann's urn was a stark contrast to the Keubeler obelisk one plot away. The cemetery workers had dug a neat rectangular hole one by two feet and three feet deep for Ann's urn. One plot for a full body could accommodate three urns. Ann was the first internment in the Whitworth plot.

This was the place Ann and I had explored as children, and now she would be interred as one more marker in Sandusky's history.

We assembled next to the opening in the ground around a small table draped in green felt with Ann's urn. My parents had left the Presbyterian Church in the late 1960s, and we had gone to a small Unitarian church growing up, but my grandmother's deep ties to the Sandusky Presbyterian Church influenced Ann. Ten years after my grandmother died, Ann decided to be married in the Sandusky Presbyterian Church and continued to go to the Presbyterian Church when she moved to Savannah. My grandmother's grave was now only a few feet away from where we were gathered.

We interred Ann's urn into the ground at the end of our stories. Now Ann's own chapter in the history of our own family was rooted in the Sandusky soil with her grandparents and great-grandparents who had been the first generation to be buried here. We took great care to use the same monument maker who had made the headstones for our grandparents to make one for Ann with the raised style of lettering. Some of my prized possessions I found in Ann's house were a few crayon drawings she had done when we were children.

■◆■◆■◆■

The next year, my mother died, and I returned to Sandusky for an eerily similar day and ceremony with the same minister and a small gathering of my wife, daughter, and two cousins.

Without knowing it, we had continued a Whitworth family tradition started a hundred years before. This was a quiet, private service to reflect on a life.

■◆■◆■◆■

Crayola's 64 Brilliant Colors continued to be a top-selling product for Binney and Smith and became the most successful, best-known brand of school crayons in the country and number one brand in the world. Since its introduction in 1958, Crayola had regularly updated their sixty-four colors, retiring a handful and introducing new ones. By 2019, Crayola's factory, still near the original stone mill in Easton Pennsylvania, produced thirteen billion crayons a year, in 120 colors, and sold in over eighty countries. The molding, labeling, and packaging is now

mostly automated. The Prang brand lives on under the Dixon Ticonderoga parent company. While they still produce crayons, they are
seldom seen among the shelves of school supplies. Prang Crayons
continues to this day as perhaps the most visible legacy of the American
Crayon Company.

■◆■◆■◆■

The year after my mother's burial at Oakland Cemetery, I returned to
Sandusky for the third consecutive year. I saw something I had not seen
since childhood. There was downtown activity on a Saturday morning.
I saw signs of rebuilding.

When I planned my visit, I wanted to be near the waterfront and
discovered the private condominiums in the massive Hinde and Dauch
paper factory on Water Street, now known as the Chesapeake Lofts.
Some of the residents offered their units online as weekend rentals, but
this was July, and all the rooms were booked. A new hotel that offered
a prime view of the waterfront had opened up nearby called the Kilbourne, which paid homage to Hector Kilbourne.

The next morning, I walked around the corner to Columbus Avenue
and the old Star Theater, which was now the Star Café. While waiting
for the café to open for the morning, I met the city manager, Eric Wobser,
and other city leaders who had a regular Saturday morning coffee klatch
in the historic building.

I stood in line and bought my coffee behind Wobser and the other
city officials. He introduced me to their informal group, and I stayed to
talk with him about what I was seeing in Sandusky. Wobser was a 1997
graduate of Thomas Edison High School in Milan, whose family roots
went back to the wave of pre-Civil War German immigrants who settled
in Sandusky. His parents were graduates of Sandusky High School. When
Wobser left for college and law school, he did so with the expectation that
he would find his future elsewhere in the big cities. After law school, he
moved to Cleveland and took a job in the mayor's office handling special
projects and later served as executive director for the historic Cleveland
neighborhood of Ohio City. But he kept Sandusky's historic limestone
buildings and innovative industrial heritage in the back of his mind.

Sandusky's commissioners had begun to re-imagine the city buildings on their historic assets. They wanted to spark something of a renaissance and reached out to Wobser. He was excited to return and bring Sandusky forward using its past. Perhaps what I was seeing was akin to the innovation of the late 1800s but instead of industry, it was in hospitality.

Wobser's idea was to make the preservation useful—to adapt it and reuse it for the present. The Chesapeake Lofts in the old Hinde and Dauch building was one of the best examples. Big cities like Pittsburgh, Buffalo, and Cleveland had had some success. Wobser touched on how small and medium Midwest cities were repurposing to reflect how people wanted to return to their cities. Without knowing it, the city had picked up where a 1951 *Sandusky Register* story profiling American Crayon concluded, "Its eyes on the future, Sandusky does not lose sight of the broad base of its uniquely important past in the development of this nation."[4]

The Sandusky Library had been at the forefront and purchased the Erie County Jail next door. The county jail itself was historic, having been built out of blue limestone in 1883. On the outside, it was an example of Gothic architecture and on the inside, it held twenty-six cells, the sheriff's residence, and included state-of-the-art chrome steel bars and safety mechanisms.

The expanded library was rededicated and opened to the public in 2004. The high ceilings and large glass windows filled the rooms with light and looked out on the County Courthouse and surrounding green space.

In addition to Chesapeake Lofts, other waterfront development moved in. The former Scott Paper Company factory site was restored as a public marina in 2011, dubbed the Paper District Marina.

Cedar Point Amusement Park, which had been an innovator in the coaster wars, reached outside the park and into the community that surrounded it. The parent company Cedar Fair bought land that had once been the site of the local airport and built a sports complex that offered baseball and soccer fields for local teams. They also teamed up with Bowling Green State University to create a co-op and classes downtown on Market Street to focus on resort and attraction management.

The Whitworth Building recalled the city's color capital history when it was designated as a local landmark and repurposed for lofts. Next door, the former Western Security Bank was renovated for city hall's administrative offices there.

In an August City Commissioners Regular Session, the commission unanimously passed a resolution to donate the salvaged American Crayon whistle to the Heritage Society of Erie County.[5]

Other signs of renewal were showing themselves. The Leaking Boot Brewing Company adopted its name from *The Boy with the Boot*, a local statue in downtown Washington Square Park. The brewery debuted Repeal Pale Ale, the first commercially produced beer in Sandusky since the Prohibition era ended in 1933. Leaking Boot added other brands to pay homage to Sandusky's brewing history, including Ohia and the Paper District Imperial Brown.

Leaking Boot knew they were picking up a lost tradition of Sandusky's German breweries. Owner Rick Semersky told *The Sandusky Register*, "Being the first brewery in town since prohibition, and our partnership with Goldhorn Brewery in Cleveland, we are helping to bring back the great brewing days of both towns, when The Cleveland-Sandusky Brewing Co. was a force across northern Ohio."[6]

■◆■◆■◆■

In 2018, Sandusky celebrated its two hundredth year as a city, the date Kilbourne's Masonic plat was officially registered with the county. At Cedar Point, a restored ballroom hosted eight hundred guests, including state and federal officials, something that harkened back to the Mad River and Lake Erie Railroad ceremony led by Oran Follett. On Sandusky Bay, tall ships sailed in on a warm July day, including a replica of the US Brig *Niagara*, Commodore Perry's relief ship during the Battle of Lake Erie. The *Niagara* replica was piloted by a professional set of officers with a ship's crew of high school students—students who would have been close in age to Oran Follett in his days as a "powder monkey" on the ship in 1813.

In a nod to Sandusky's innovative foundries, LEWCO, a local maker of industrial equipment, welded a metal art installation, forming "1818," the founding year of Sandusky. The company's two most experienced welders created the piece that was later donated to be displayed in the newly designated Paper District Marina on West Shoreline Drive. Abolitionist Rush Sloane's Italianate home was undergoing a full restoration, and the Erie County Historical Society initiated an Underground Railroad walking tour stopping at the homes of Thomas Beecher, Rush Sloane, and Joseph Root.

The city also used the bicentennial to unveil plans for more public art spaces that included a fountain filled with illuminated cylinders representing crayons. The concept was meant to pay homage to the inventiveness of the American Crayon Company.

Other recognition followed with Sandusky being named by *USA Today* in a 2019 reader's poll as the Best Small Coastal Town.[7]

Social media sites dedicated to Sandusky show a strong following of current and former residents who reminisce about growing up in the area. Posts about American Crayon consistently attracted dozens of likes and fond recollections usually about family members who worked there. A typical post read "This was a great place to work! It was mostly family members working there. My grandfather, my mom, my aunt, me, and my uncle."

■◆■◆■◆■

I finished my coffee with Eric Wobser at the Star Café and got up to leave, but I paused to exchange business cards. I told him I was honestly excited to see what was happening and would look forward to visiting again. On my walk back to the Kilbourne Hotel, I stopped and bought a copy of *The Sandusky Register*, taking in the view of the State Theater, the Cedar Point Ferry, and Sandusky Bay.

When I called Eric about a year later and asked how the renewal was going, he told me he was sitting in the new city offices overlooking Washington Park.

■◆■◆■◆■

Epilogue

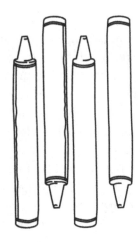

*History written in pencil is easily
erased, but crayon is forever.*

—Emilie Autumn

MY MYTHOLOGY OF the *Color Capital of the World* would not exist without the Sunday night stories at the dinner table as told by my grandmother and the packets of crayons she gave as presents. I could not have made pilgrimages to these destinations unless others had moved away. First it was my great-grandfather, John Whitworth, who died before he could move to Pasadena. When my turn came, I moved from Sandusky to Washington, DC. Maybe I should call it not a move, but a migration.

Sandusky was where I was born and where I grew up. My ancestors had embraced the town's era of invention to build the Color Capital of the World. The city was the source of my mythology and I had rediscovered it. Three months after my mother was buried in Oakland Cemetery, my father died and was interred at Arlington National Cemetery, ten minutes from my house. I had sorted, cataloged, and carted around rooms full of crayon-created family artifacts, and now I felt like the last ship left sailing the ocean with a cargo full of relics from generations of Sandusky families.

I have lived more of my life away from Sandusky than in it, but I still felt tied to the skeletons of the past, to the memory of the crayon factory and the Midwest—to the small towns of Ohio. The attachment can be as simple as seeing an eight-pack of crayons in the local drugstore, even if the brand on the box is no longer American Crayons.

Maybe it is a romantic illusion that the wealth of the crayon should have created a permanent home for our family, like Henry Ford had done in nearby Detroit or, better still, an English family estate held by a succession of lords for eight hundred years. What kind of mythology and personal satisfaction would that bring?

But in America, permanence is the exception, and we tend not to stay in one place longer than a few generations. We become restless and move on. Jonathan Whitworth, Warren Cowdery, and William Curtis moved west from the eastern states. My great-grandfather and grandfather sought to move from Ohio to California. There was no crayon legacy to carry on except to complete my sister's and mother's wishes to inter their remains in the family plot. When I moved away from Ohio, in the opposite direction, east toward the mid-Atlantic, toward what I thought would be a more secure future, I was turning away from risk—unlike my great-grandfather.

Looking ahead, I now wonder what will happen to my daughter when she starts to make her way in the world. Where will she want to go? Will she move? And if she does, will she look for her mythology? Will she want to return to the place where she grew up or explore the places that her ancestors called home?

Looking back, I think we unconsciously spend the first half of life absorbing our hometowns and mythologies, and the second half trying to understand them.

As I write, Sandusky's resurgence may be uncertain. The historic State Theater was badly damaged from a severe storm that swept through the downtown with restoration plans underway. Even so, there will be future mythologies to create. I will have to wait to find out what my daughter draws from the past and what she leaves behind. Crayons will probably be a faint idea to her. Maybe she will write her own book, carrying the thread backward and forward, knitting the past and present together. The sequel, as for all following generations, may be my daughter looking for the threads of her own identity and mythology.

One thing I learned in the search for the spark that created the Color Capital days is that there is no permanence. Build. Boom. Bust. And now transformation to something new.

The capital has moved on and may be claimed by others. I was driven by the memories of people and places, but the people and places were gone, and more would disappear every day. The prosperity of the color capital did not last three generations. In the nursing home my mother repeated herself from years ago that she was never told she had to worry about money. Even if she had, the American Crayon Company and its legacy would probably not have lasted. The Crayon Capital of the World had moved on.

I suppose the journey led me to learn what has been known for ages: the only permanence is change. What remains is the desire to hold on to the memories of others. It was an ancient urge to remember and pass down the stories.

One other thing I learned: my favorite color is blue.

Sources

Color Capital of the World is a blend of history and memoir that combines sources of memory and artifacts. In addition to my own memory, background about the Cowdery, Curtis, and Whitworth families comes from our family's collection of photographs and letters. I was especially grateful to interview my third cousin, Marty Longer, for details about the Curtis and Whitworth families. I have tried to reconstruct those personal events as accurately as possible. For history of the American Crayon Company, I was fortunate to have a collection of material, much of it passed down, including company correspondence, product catalogs, promotional literature, photographs, stock certificates, and company letterhead. I also drew upon other company-produced material, including a 1964 booklet, *The American Crayon Company: The Story of "a Crayon and How It Grew,"* prepared as part of an Industrial Recognition Dinner. *The All-American*, an internal American Crayon Company newsletter, provided company news, information about managers and employees, and new products (a collection of *The All-American* is also held by the Sandusky Library Research Center). Part of my collection also includes the company's longest-running publication, *Everyday Art: News and Comments on the Future of School and Industrial Arts,* Volumes 1–48 (1922–1970), and provided history of the company's promotion of art in the schools as well as insights about the personalities that led the movement. In particular, the 1935 "Centennial" issue provided stories about the company's innovation and development of new products. Published in 1996, Brenda Elliot's *The Best of Its Kind: Since 1795: The Incredible American Heritage of the Dixon Ticonderoga Company* provided an excellent overview of the company's founding, the development of crayons, and its integration into Dixon Ticonderoga. Ed Welter deserves special mention as a source for company history. He has maintained a crayon collecting website since 2001 that provides extensively documented histories on crayon companies and was especially useful in cataloging every product produced by researching American Crayon as well as its competition with rival companies. My correspondence with him also proved valuable in understanding the crayon business of the twentieth century. Other details about the company's history came from conversations and correspondence with Ron Davidson, Special Collections Librarian, Sandusky Library (Ron was also an excellent source for confirming details about Sandusky history generally). The Smithsonian National Museum also provided American Crayon Company promotional brochures from its Binney & Smith collection (labeled competitor "research"). In addition, correspondence with former employees and their family members provided first-hand details of life at the factory. Ben Baker, whose grandfather, Irvin Baker, was one of the last employees at the factory, provided valuable details about the last days of the factory's operation.

For the history of Sandusky, Ohio, I was fortunate to have inherited a small library of books that proved valuable, including three by Charles E. Frohman: *A History of Sandusky and Erie County* and *Sandusky Potpourri*, as well as *Rebels on Lake Erie*. For details about the Battle of Lake Erie and descriptions of natural surroundings of Sandusky Bay, I consulted Harry Ross's book, *Enchanting Isles of Erie*. For the early history of Sandusky, I relied principally on Hewson Peeke's two-volume *Standard History of Erie County, Ohio* and Ernst von Schulenburg's *Sandusky Then and Now*. For stories of prominent places and people in Sandusky's history, I used a variety of sources, including Ellie Damm's *Treasure by the Bay: The Historic Architecture of Sandusky, Ohio*; Ron Davidson's *Sandusky Ohio*; Helen Hansen's *At Home in Early Biebow*; Natascha and Steven Salerno's *The Crayon Man: The True Story of the*

Invention of Crayola Crayons; and *The History of Crayons*, https:// arthearty.com/crayons-history.

Helen M. Hansen's *Sandusky, Foundations for the Future*, published in Sandusky in 1975, as well as her work with Virginia F. Steinmann, *From the Widow's Walk: A View of Sandusky* provided critical background on Sandusky's history. For the history of the Lake Shore Railway, details came from Harry Christiansen's *Lake Shore Electric Railway: 1893–1938*. In addition, the online resources of *The Sandusky Register*, the Sandusky Library online Historical Collection, the Sandusky History blog, and the Erie County Historical Society provided additional historic detail.

For the history of crayons, I relied principally on Ed Welter's Crayon Collecting website, which is perhaps the single best guide to crayons available. This was supplemented with history from Brenda Elliott's *The Best of Its Kind*, and ArtHearty.com. For additional history of Binney & Smith's development of crayons, a useful book was Natascha Biebow's *The Crayon Man: The True Story of the Invention of Crayola Crayons*.

Notes

Introduction

1. Deane B. Judd and Günter Wyszecki, *Color in Business, Science, and Industry*, Wiley Series in Pure and Applied Optics (New York: Wiley-Interscience, 1975), 388.
2. "What Are the Most Common School Colors of Universities?" *Reference*, updated March 27, 2020, https://www.reference.com/world-view/common-school-colors-universities-ade34025919976be.
3. Sarah Cascone, "The First Blue Pigment Discovered in 200 Years Is Finally Commercially Available. Here's Why It Already Has a Loyal Following," *Art World*, January 14, 2021, https://news.artnet.com/art-world/yinmn-blue-comes-market-1921665.
4. A partial list of family members selected for the individuals featured in the story.

Chapter 1

1. Ed Welter, "American Crayon Company, Sandusky, OH: 1835–1957," Crayoncollecting.com, accessed January 2, 2022, http://www.crayoncollecting.com/Other/AmericanCrayon.htm. Ed Welter, of Portland, Oregon, offered detailed inventories of crayons packages, company histories, and tips on how to display and present crayon collections. Welter painstaking noted some 2,929 different colors of crayon had been named over the years.
2. "To Workers Hit by Factory Closures, 'This NAFTA Thing Was a Disaster,'" *The Toledo Blade*, October 9, 2016, Insurance News Net, https://insurancenewsnet.com/oarticle/to-workers-hit-by-factory-closures-this-nafta-thing-was-a-disaster.

Chapter 2

1. American Crayon Company promotional publication 1972–73, part of the author's personal collection.
2. Wendy Solomon, "From Cro-Magnon to Crayon: A Colorful History," *The Morning Call*, October 5, 2003, https://www.mcall.com/news/mc-xpm-2003-10-05-3512966-story.html.

3. "Sumptuary Laws Regulate Luxury," *The Encyclopedia of Fashion*, http://www. fashionencyclopedia.com/fashion_costume_culture/The-Ancient-World-Rome/ Sumptuary-Laws-Regulate-Luxury.html; Hannah Foskett, "A History of the Colour Purple," https://www.artsandcollections.com/a-history-of-the-colour-purple/.

4. For example, see Kassia St. Clair, *The Secret Lives of Color* (New York: Penguin Books, 2017).

5. Much of the crayon history follows Ed Welter's article on the history of crayons, http://www.crayoncollecting.com/hoco1.htm.

6. "Louis Prang, Father of the American Christmas Card," New York Historical Society Museum & Library, blog.nyhistory.org/prang.

7. Brenda Elliot, *The Best of Its Kind: Since 1795: The Incredible American Heritage of the Dixon Ticonderoga Company* (Heathrow, FL: Dixon Ticonderoga Company, 1996), 248.

8. Brenda Elliot, *The Best of Its Kind*, 249.

9. Natascha Biebow and Steven Salerno, *The Crayon Man: The True Story of the Invention of Crayola Crayons* (Boston and New York, Houghton Mifflin Harcourt, 2019). See also *The History of Crayons*, https://arthearty.com/crayons-history.

10. American Crayon Company promotional publication 1972–73, author's personal collection.

11. "Ken Nordine—Fuller Paint "Color" Spots (circa. 1964)," *Audio Arcana*, https:// audioarcana.blogspot.com/2016/03/ken-nordine-fuller-paint-color-spots.html.

12. A composite of my own recollection; the blog above can also be viewed as a YouTube recording (three-minute mark) at https://youtu.be/bkePKo82nfM.

Chapter 3

1. Charles Frohman, *A History of Sandusky and Erie County* (Columbus: The Ohio Historical Society, 1965), 2–3.

2. Writers' Program of the WPA, *Lake Erie Vacationland in Ohio: A Guide to Sandusky Bay Region* (Ohio State Archeological and Historical Society, Columbus, OH, 1941).

3. Article VI of the ordinance. The history surrounding the ordinance was described in David McCullough, *The Pioneers: The Heroic Story of the Settlers Who Brought the American Ideal West* (New York: Simon and Schuster, 2019).

4. Harry H. Ross, *Enchanting Isles of Erie: Historic Sketches of Romantic Battle of Lake Erie* (H. H. Ross, 1949), 9–12.

5. Later, Huron County was divided into two counties, with Erie County being the second county.

6. *Powder Monkey* is a nineteenth-century naval term of art for a young sailor who carried gunpowder from the powder in the ship's hold to the artillery pieces.

7. Helen Hansen, *At Home in Early Sandusky: Foundations for the Future* (Sandusky, OH: 1975), 1.

8. Named after General Mad Anthony Wayne, who was hugely popular in Ohio at the time for winning the Battle of the Fallen Timbers (near present day Toledo) in 1784 against the Shawnee Nation, effectively ending the Northwest Indian War in Ohio.

9. B. A. Hinsdale, *The Old Northwest* (New York: Townsend, 1888), 389–90.

10. Charles Dickens, *American Notes: A Journey* (New York: Fromm International Publishing, 1985), 196.

11. Dickens, *American Notes*, 197.
12. Dickens, *American Notes*, 197.
13. "Lincoln's Death Mourned in Sandusky," Erie County Ohio History, accessed January 8, 2022, https://www.eriecountyohiohistory.com/content/uploads/2018/12/1865-April-Lincoln-shot.pdf.
14. Ari Hoogenboom, *Rutherford B. Hayes: Warrior and President* (Lawrence: University of Kansas Press, 1995), 294.

Chapter 4
1. Frohman, *A History of Sandusky and Erie County*, 48–49, and author's personal collection of Cowdery/Curtis family records.
2. Helen Hansen and Virginia Steinemann, *From the Widow's Walk: A View of Sandusky* (Sandusky, OH: Follett House Museum, Branch of the Sandusky Library, 1991), 9.
3. William Curtis's history is from the author's personal collection of Cowdery/Curtis family records.
4. *Everyday Art: The American Crayon Company Hundredth Anniversary* 13, no. 3 (February–March 1935): 18–19.

Chapter 5
1. I learned later that the study and collection of stock and bond certificates is called *scripophily*, a specialized field of numismatics, collected for the artistic and historical value of the documents. Some certificates are prized for their engravings.
2. Hewson L. Peeke, *A Standard History of Erie County, Ohio*, 2 vols. (Chicago and New York: Lewis Publishing Company, 1916), 1205. The two-volume set runs close to two thousand pages. In an odd coincidence, the biography immediately before John Whitworth is for Christian Kropf (no known relation). In 1957, my parents Walter Kropf and Mary Whitworth, were married; over fifty years after the history was published.
3. Though my great-grandfather and grandfather were both John Whitworth, they were not technically Senior and Junior because my great-grandfather did not have a middle name and my grandfather had the middle name Curtis.
4. Frohman, *Sandusky Potpourri*, item 79.
5. Colleen Dunn Bates et al., *Hometown Pasadena: The Insider's Guide* (Pasadena: Prospect Park Books, 2006), 33.
6. Author's personal collection of Whitworth/Curtis family papers.
7. Peeke, *A Standard History of Erie County, Ohio*, 1205–6.
8. Welter, http://www.crayoncollecting.com/hoco7.htm.
9. Welter, http://www.crayoncollecting.com/hoco7.htm.
10. Elliott, *The Best of Its Kind*, 252–253.
11. Ad found in *The National School Digest: The Educational Review of Books* 41, no. 1 (September 1921), https://books.google.com/books/about/The_School_Executive.html?id=hm9LAAAAYAAJ.
12. Elliot W. Eisner and Michael D. Day, eds., *Handbook of Research and Policy in Art Education* (Mahwah, NJ; London: Lawrence Erlbaum Associates, 2004).
13. "Ford, Henry," https://www.encyclopedia.com/people/social-sciences-and-law/business-leaders/henry-ford.
14. *The Firelands Pioneer*, The Firelands Historical Society, January 1921, Norwalk, OH, 775.

15. "The People's Choice," *Life Magazine*, November 11, 1940.

16. Ugo Giannini and Maxine Giannini, *Drawing D-Day: An Artist's Journey Through War* (Mineola, NY: Dover Publications, 2019).

17. "American Crayon Company Is Sandusky's Oldest Industry," *Sandusky Register*, November 9, 1956, https://www.newspapers.com/clip/787399/american-crayon-1956-overview-of-accs/.

18. "City of Sandusky Commissioners—Regular Session," August 14, 2017, http://www.ci.sandusky.oh.us/CC%20Agendas/CC%20Minutes/8.14.17%20CC%20Minutes.pdf.

Chapter 6

1. "History of Oakland Cemetery," City of Sandusky, https://www.ci.sandusky.oh.us/residents/public_services/history.php.

Chapter 7

1. "Did Howard Hughes' Will End Up on an Ohio Beach?" *The Columbus Dispatch*, July 4, 2012, https://www.dispatch.com/story/news/2012/07/04/did-howard-hughes-will-end/24007066007/.

Chapter 9

1. Thanks to Ben Baker at: https://www.cbgitty.com/the-american-crayon-company/.

2. Elliott, *The Best of Its Kind*.

3. "Color Historic Plant Gone," *Toledo Blade*, December 12, 2002 https://www.toledoblade.com/local/2002/12/12/Color-historic-plant-gone/stories/200212120079.

4. "Arson Suspected in Boeckling Fire," *Sandusky Register*, June 22, 1989, https://newspaperarchive.com/sandusky-register-jun-22-1989-p-1/.

5. MARKO and JHONO, "American Crayon Factory: Abandoned and Now Gone," video, 9:46, https://youtu.be/nJiQRWoxoXU.

Chapter 11

1. US Census 1970 and 2000.

2. "Charges Dropped Against Ohio Park Mower," June 9, 2009, *Columbus Dispatch*, https://www.dispatch.com/story/news/2009/06/09/charges-dropped-against-ohio-park/23401826007/.

3. Adam Rowe, "If the Adult Coloring Book Craze Is Dead, It Needs A Postmortem," *Forbes*, May 21, 2018, https://www.forbes.com/sites/adamrowe1/2018/05/31/if-the-adult-coloring-book-craze-is-dead-it-needs-a-postmortem/?sh=62a2e69e7dae.

4. "American Crayon Company Is Sandusky's Oldest Industry," *Sandusky Register*, 33.

5. "City of Sandusky Commissioners—Regular Session," August 14, 2017.

6. "On tap: First business-brewed beer in Sandusky since Prohibition Era," https://sanduskyregister.com/news/10019/on-tap-first-business-brewed-beer-in-sandusky-since-prohibition-era/. Leaking Boot went out of business in 2020. Two more microbreweries were operating in downtown Sandusky.

7. "Award-Winning Coastal Small Towns Where You Can Get Away from It All," https://www.usatoday.com/picture-gallery/travel/10best/awards/2020/09/01/10-best-coastal-small-towns-us-venice-florida-sandusky-ohio/5621252002/.

Selected Bibliography

Biebow, Natascha and Steven Salerno. *The Crayon Man: The True Story of the Invention of Crayola Crayons*. Boston and New York, Houghton Mifflin Harcourt, 2019.

Christiansen, Harry. *Lake Shore Electric Railway: 1893–1938*. Cleveland, OH: Self-published, 1963.

Damm, Ellie. *Treasure by the Bay: The Historic Architecture of Sandusky, Ohio*, Western Reserve Historical Society Publication, 1989.

Davidson, Ron. *Sandusky Ohio*. Chicago: Arcadia Publishing, 2002.

Elliot, Brenda. *The Best of Its Kind: Since 1795: The Incredible American Heritage of the Dixon Ticonderoga Company*. Heathrow, FL: The Dixon Ticonderoga Company, 1996.

Frohman, Charles E. *Rebels on Lake Erie*. Rutherford B. Hayes Presidential Center, 1977.

Frohman, Charles. *A History of Sandusky and Erie County*. Columbus: The Ohio Historical Society, 1974.

Frohman, Charles. *Sandusky Potpourri*. Columbus: The Ohio Historical Society, 1974. The third of a series of three pamphlets containing short articles based on articles from early issues of *The Sandusky Register*.

Hansen, Helen. *At Home in Early Sandusky: Foundations for the Future*, 1975. Based on the columns she wrote titled "Stately Old Homes," which were published by *The Sandusky Register* in 1958 and 1959, as well as other pieces.

Hansen, Helen M., and Virginia F. Steinmann. *From the Widow's Walk: A View of Sandusky*. Sandusky, OH: Follett House Museum, Branch of the Sandusky Library, 1991.

"History of Crayons, The." Art Hearty. https://arthearty.com/crayons-history.

Hoogenboom, Ari. *Rutherford B. Hayes: Warrior and President.* Lawrence: University of Kansas Press, 1995.

Peeke, Hewson L. *A Standard History of Erie County, Ohio.* 2 vols. Chicago and New York: Lewis Publishing Company, 1916.

Ross, Harry H. *Enchanting Isles of Erie: Historic Sketches of Romantic Battle of Lake Erie, Oliver Hazard Perry. Put-in-Bay, Lakeside, Kelleys Island, Middle Bass, Johnson's Island, Catawba, North Bass, Cedar Point, Sandusky, Port Clinton, other Islands and Resorts.* H. H. Ross, 1949.

Seibert, Wilbur H. *The Underground Railroad from Slavery to Freedom: A Comprehensive History.* Dover edition, 2006. https://www.gutenberg.org/files/49038/49038-h/49038-h.htm.

Von Schulenburg, Ernst. *Sandusky Then and Now.* Translated into English by Marion Cleaveland Lange and Norbert Adolph Lange. Publication No. 115 of the Western Reserve Historical Society, 1959.

Online Resources

Crayon Collecting website, maintained by Ed Welter, http://crayoncollecting.com/about.htm.

The Sandusky Register, https://sanduskyregister.com/.

Sandusky Library online Historical Collection, https://www.sanduskylib.org/using-the-library/special-collections/.

Online Sandusky History blog, https://sanduskyhistory.blogspot.com/.

Erie County Historical Society, https://www.eriecountyohiohistory.com/.

Acknowledgments

The history of the American Crayon Company belongs to the thousands of its employees and their families who worked there during the company's 167-year existence. This story is in no way the definitive one, but it is sincere and heartfelt for a time and place that affected many lives for the better. In researching this book, I came into contact with lost relatives and met former employees and their families. My thanks to third cousins "Punky" Porto and Marty Longer and her husband Ted. Marty and Ted were especially gracious in hosting a lunch during which they shared their stories about Earl Curtis and his tenure as president of the company and shared crayon company memorabilia. Of the former employees and their families, I am especially grateful to Ben Baker and his grandfather Irvin Baker. Irvin was one of the last employees at the American Crayon Company factory before it was shuttered. Ben shared the stories his grandfather told about his time there and, through his grandfather's foresight, rescued many valuable artifacts from the factory that would have otherwise been lost in the demolition—some of which Ben graciously shared with me. Thanks to Mary Rice, who worked at the factory in the 1960s and agreed to share her experience with me in a phone conversation.

Thanks also to a wonderful network of writing friends who encouraged, coached, read, and proofed different drafts: Kathryn Sulzbaugh, Sally Dilgart, Anne Fealey, Dayna Harpster, Mary Bencivengo, and

Barbara Esstman. Rebecca Davis was especially helpful in her attention to the details of fine writing and helped improve the story. Thank you to Anne Trubek of Cleveland's Belt Publishing. Her book proposal course provided a valuable forum on how to structure a book proposal.

I also owe my thanks to Sandusky historians and subject matter experts Ron Davidson at the Sandusky Library and Tom Horsman, Communications Manager of the City of Sandusky, as well as Kristina Smith, author of Lost Sandusky and Communications and Marketing Manager at Rutherford B. Hayes Presidential Library and Museums. Special thanks to City Manager, Eric Wobser, a bright light for Sandusky, for his time and willingness to talk with me about city's future. I am indebted to long-time *Sandusky Register* photographer, Tim Fleck for photographing the last days factory shortly before its demolition and for giving me permission to use one of his photos in the book.

On crayon knowledge, Ed Welter is truly the King of crayons with his endless knowledge and hundreds of hours of research. His site on crayon collecting is perhaps the best source on the topic.

I am deeply grateful to Jon Stephen Miller, Director at the University of Akron Press who agreed to take on the book and members of the Editorial Review Board who provided valuable input. Also, thanks to Thea Ledendecker, Editor and Business Manager at the Press, for her experience and patience in guiding me through the detailed process of preparing a manuscript for book production. And thanks to the artistic skill of Amy Freels, Editorial and Design Coordinator at the Press, for an amazing cover. And the very helpful Julie Gammon, Marketing Manager at the Press who had a wealth of great suggestions and patiently responded to my many emails about the process.

Last, thank you to my wife Eileen, who was a captive audience whenever I needed feedback or encouragement. She also had to navigate the piles of books and research material that took over our dining room. And thanks to my bibliophile daughter, Charlotte, who encouraged me to write and tried her best to coach me on Chicago Style citations.

Any errors of fact or mistakes are mine alone.

John Kropf is the author of *Unknown Sands: Journeys Around the World's Most Isolated Country*, which *Publishers Weekly* praised as a fascinating narrative bound to hook adventurers. His writing has appeared in *The Baltimore Sun*, *Florida Sun-Sentinel*, *The Washington Post*, and elsewhere. Kropf was born in Sandusky and raised in Erie County, Ohio. He is an attorney in the Washington, DC, area.